WALKS IN THE SOUTH DOWNS NATIONAL PARK

About the Author

Kev Reynolds is a freelance author, photojournalist and lecturer whose first guide for Cicerone Press appeared in 1978. Although his work regularly takes him to some of the world's most spectacular mountains, he is passionate about the more homely landscapes of southern England, and especially the South Downs, which he visits at every opportunity. A member of the Alpine Club, Austrian Alpine Club and the Outdoor Writers and Photographers Guild, Kev has walked, trekked or climbed in the Alps, Bhutan, Nepal, North Africa, Norway, Peru, the Pyrenees, Russia, Sikkim and Turkey. His love of the outdoors was kindled almost before he could walk; it has been his life's motivation and reward and he regularly travels throughout Britain to share that enthusiasm through his lectures. Check him out on www.kevreynolds.co.uk.

Other Cicerone Guides by the author

The North Downs Way
The South Downs Way
The Cotswold Way
Walking in Sussex
Walking in Kent
Walking in the Alps
Trekking in the Alps
100 Hut Walks in the Alps
Tour of the Oisans: GR54
Tour of the Vanoise
Tour of Mont Blanc
Tour of the Jungfrau Region
Alpine Pass Route
Chamonix to Zermatt:
    The Walker's Haute Route

Écrins National Park
Walking in Austria
Walks in the Engadine
Walking in the Valais
The Bernese Alps
Ticino – Switzerland
Central Switzerland
Walks and Climbs in the Pyrenees
The Pyrenees
Annapurna: a Trekker's Guide
Everest: a Trekker's Guide
Langtang, Helambu & Gosainkund:
    a Trekker's Guide
Kangchenjunga: a Trekker's Guide
Manaslu: a Trekker's Guide

WALKS IN THE SOUTH DOWNS NATIONAL PARK

by

Kev Reynolds

CICERONE

2 POLICE SQUARE, MILNTHORPE, CUMBRIA LA7 7PY
www.cicerone.co.uk

© Kev Reynolds 2011
First edition 2011

ISBN 978 1 85284 618 3

A catalogue record for this book is available from the British Library.

Printed by KHL Printing, Singapore.
All photographs by Kev and Linda Reynolds.

Dedication

This book is dedicated to all who worked so hard, for so long, to make the South Downs a National Park

Acknowledgements

Those of us who walk on the South Downs owe a debt of gratitude to generations of landowners who tended this cherished landscape with loving care; to those who fought for so long to have it recognised as a National Park, among them countless individuals (too numerous to mention by name), as well as the South Downs Campaign, Council for National Parks, The Ramblers, CPRE, and Hilary Benn MP who, as Environment Secretary, finally gave the go-ahead for it to become England's 10th National Park after more than 60 years of longing. On a more personal note, I am grateful to local enthusiasts and unnamed historians whose booklets and leaflets, often on sale in village churches, provided useful background information to some of the areas visited. Our good friend Maggie Dilley accompanied us on several of these walks to add to our enjoyment, but as ever it was my wife who shared every mile, every smile and every view, and whose loving support made the research and writing of this book such an enriching experience. I'm also grateful to Jonathan Williams for his eagerness to add this guide to the Cicerone list, and to his production team (Lois, Neil, Caroline and Clare and editor James Deboo) whose skills, talents and friendship are all treasured.

Kev Reynolds

Front cover: The Seven Sisters from Seaford Head (Walk 7)

CONTENTS

An airy clifftop view of Beachy Head lighthouse (Walk 1)

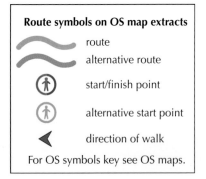

Route symbols on OS map extracts

route

alternative route

start/finish point

alternative start point

direction of walk

For OS symbols key see OS maps.

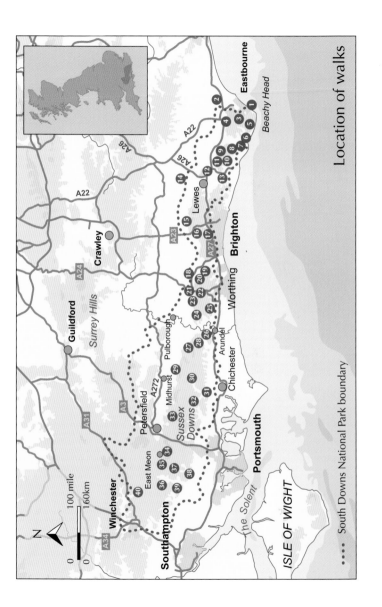

Location of walks

····· South Downs National Park boundary

Descending the north flank of Edburton Hill (Walk 16)

INTRODUCTION

The quintessential Downs: the eastern Downs, from above Wilmington

The sum of the whole is this: walk and be happy; walk and be healthy. The best way to lengthen out our days is to walk steadily and with a purpose.

Charles Dickens
(1812–1870)

A few days ago we walked the last of the routes for this book. The forecast was not promising; the late summer sky was heavy with impatient clouds, and rain fell as the Downs hove into view. But half an hour into our walk the cloud cover broke, and sunshine swept the great open spaces like searchlights picking out individual features before moving on. It was mid-week and we had the world to ourselves – plus a few hundred sheep and skylarks that hung as tiny specks over our heads hour upon blustery hour.

We walked southward, the distant sea speckled with white. In one direction a harvested field had been rolled into pillows of golden straw; in another cropped grasslands stretched into infinity. The spire of an ancient church beckoned from a wooded hollow, and as we wandered down the slope to investigate, we

11

ate our fill of sweet, juicy blackberries and breathed in the fragrance of honeysuckle.

The church was a gem. For over a thousand years it had marked the hopes and aspirations, the joys and sorrows, new life and tearful parting, of countless generations of South Downs folk. Its carved arches caught our breath with wonder. Its windows cast patterns on a floor worn by prayerful knees; its walls echoed the peace of ten centuries and more. On a memorial tablet we discovered a verse that struck a chord, so perfectly did it sum up what the World Out There meant to us. It could become our epitaph.

At a junction of paths just below the crown of a hill but sheltered from the wind, we settled on the grass to eat our sandwiches with a panoramic view of something like 300° to gaze upon. A local woman exercising her dogs stopped to pass the time of day, to share enthusiasm (hers and ours) for the beauty of the scene, for the enriching goodness of the Downs, for the freedom and energy to be able to enjoy them. If anything, her appreciation increased ours and we parted with smiles of friendship.

Having crossed and recrossed the Downs we arrived back where we'd begun several hours earlier, and now gazed northward across the Weald – the Weald patterned with field and meadow, blotches of woodland, a few tiny villages, and more hills far off and blue with distance.

In a little over a month we'll be in the Himalaya among sky-scratching

The walk across the Seven Sisters is a much-loved outing (Walk 5)

Some of England's loveliest villages are found in the South Downs; this thatched cottage is in Amberley (Walk 24)

peaks and tumbling glaciers. But it'll be no more beautiful or rewarding than our days wandering on the South Downs. Just different. The 'blunt, bow-headed, whalebacked Downs' are no substitute for bigger hills. Complete in themselves, they're enriching, fulfilling, uplifting, and anyone who enjoys a walk with a big broad view and the brush of an unchecked breeze will find all they need here.

This book is a guide to some of the most rewarding walks to be had in the South Downs National Park, and is the result of many years spent exploring these lovely hills, valleys and villages. Literally hundreds of miles have been walked, in all seasons and in all weathers, and we've enjoyed every one of them. The difficulty was in choosing just 40 routes to represent the essential Downs.

THE ESSENTIAL DOWNS

The Weald is good, the Downs are best –
I'll give you the run of 'em, East to West.

Rudyard Kipling
(1865–1936)

These smooth green hills stretch for about 90 miles from Beachy Head near Eastbourne to St Catherine's Hill, overlooking the River Itchen, at Winchester: an ample, generous land characterised by skylarks, cowslips, poppies and sheep. Angled slightly inland away from the coast, the narrow band rising above Eastbourne broadens into sometimes heavily wooded, parallel ridges further west, while nestling in their folds lie ancient churches and villages of flint, half-timbered brickwork and thatch, some owing their history to estates like Firle, Goodwood and Parham which today preserve large areas of unspoilt grassland.

Kipling was right when he said that the Weald is good, the Downs are best, and millions of visitors a year would probably echo that sentiment, for hills are more seductive than plains and valleys, and the South Downs have a subtle beauty that defies comparison with bigger hills and mountains. Size plays no part in their attraction; after all, the highest Down is only 886ft. Puny, you might think; just a wart, a pimple. But it forms part of a larger whole; a cherished landscape, in perspective as impressive as many a mountain range, and every bit as beautiful.

Anyone who loves open space, an unchecked breeze and a long view will find the Downs rewarding. 'Hills roll on after hills, till the last and largest hides those that succeed behind it,' wrote Richard Jefferies in *Nature Near London*. In countless places no buildings are visible, only hills and valleys – a land without limits under an immense sky. Walking alone up there one can enjoy solitude, although some may find it a little intimidating. Dr Johnson did. He thought the sense of isolation enough to make a man want to hang himself, if he could only find a tree. But many more will welcome the peace and lack of people as invigorating.

There is no wild nature on the South Downs. This is a man-made landscape, and history has left its mark on almost every mile, beginning with primitive Stone Age settlers who grazed sheep, cattle and pigs here before the last Ice Age. A few of their long barrows (communal tombs) remain, and at Cissbury the ground is rucked with the pits and spoil heaps of a Neolithic flint mine; some crude flint implements were also discovered at Slindon.

Many hundreds of *tumuli* (round barrows) in which Bronze Age people buried their dead line the ridgeway, and at the head of several dry valleys are cross-dykes, reminders of the same period. These may have been part of a defence system to protect routes across open land, or were used perhaps as the boundaries of agricultural estates.

Hillforts, such as those on Mount Caburn, Devil's Dyke and Old Winchester Hill, proclaim the one-time presence of Iron Age man, but none is more impressive than Cissbury Ring, a massive earthwork covering 65 acres. Although the site had been mined for flint in the New Stone Age, Iron Age settlers built their fortification here some time between 300BC and 59BC, with two clearly defined ramparts and a protective ditch from which around 60,000 tons of chalk had to be dug.

The knowledge of how to smelt iron had reached Britain prior to 500BC, but when Belgic tribes arrived sometime around 100BC, they used this knowledge to create a heavy wheeled plough with which they turned the downland soil, creating in the process lynchets (or field systems) whose rippled evidence can be seen today all along the Downs. The wheeled plough revolutionised agriculture to such an extent that it is said to have dominated the region until the arrival of the Romans in AD43.

Under Roman rule, Chichester (*Noviomagus*) became the regional capital, with the construction of Stane Street around AD70 being the major link, for both military and economic purposes, with London (*Londinium*) some 56 miles away. This was a major feat of engineering, for the road was metalled, had a camber, and climbed over the steep-sided Downs between Chichester and Pulborough. Sections of this road are still clearly visible across Bignor Hill, while an important estate was sited at the foot of the Downs outside Bignor village. In 1811 a mosaic of a dancing girl was unearthed here by a plough, prompting excavations which revealed the site of a large and luxurious fourth-century Roman villa. Farmsteads and country houses built around the same time have also been discovered along the foot of the Downs.

By the time the Saxons arrived, landing around AD477 somewhere between Beachy Head and Selsey Bill, the South Downs had been farmed for more than 2000 years, but unlike their predecessors these newcomers preferred to work the valleys spreading into the Weald, where the soil was better watered and more productive. It was the Saxons who cleared large swathes of woodland and created drove roads to connect the scattered parishes in which they built their simple churches. Some of these still stand, like that of St Andrew's at Bishopstone, while others that were modified numerous times through the centuries retain Saxon features, such as the stumpy tower at Jevington.

Following the Norman Conquest much of the region was divided into 'rapes', each of which controlled a strip of coast, an area of downland for grazing, farmland for cultivation, and a section of Wealden forest for hunting. The Normans built castles at Arundel and Lewes, and aided the spread of Christianity by erecting many more solid-looking churches which add character to the villages they serve.

Over the following two or three centuries the population grew, communities expanded, market towns were established and sheep grazing dominated the Downs, while cornfields spread along their base. Reaching a peak in the 18th century, it is estimated that some 400,000 ewes grazed the Sussex Downs, their fleeces being worked into cloth by Wealden woolmasters, or sold across the Channel to merchants in Flanders.

Although the Downs escaped the ravages of the industrial revolution, food shortages and high prices during the Napoleonic Wars spurred local sheep farmers to return to the plough. When food prices fell, much of the land was restored to pasture, until the First World War once again called for greater food production. With higher yields resulting from improved fertilisers there was no going back, and in the Second World War the extent of this cultivation increased even more.

It was this destruction of traditional downland that effectively blocked the 1947 proposal by Sir Arthur Hobhouse for the South Downs to become one of England's first National Parks. While several other areas included in his report gained National Park status, in 1956 the South Downs was rejected on the grounds that its recreational value had been 'considerably reduced by extensive cultivation'. Instead, two Areas of Outstanding Natural Beauty were established: the Sussex Downs and East Hampshire AONBs.

But walkers were unimpressed by official rejection. Voting with their feet they were drawn in greater numbers to explore the region when, in 1972, its 'recreational value' was enhanced by the establishment of the South Downs Way between Eastbourne and Buriton on the Sussex–Hampshire border. Designated an official long distance route by the Countryside Commission, the SDW was the first in Britain to be both a footpath and bridleway. Today this increasingly popular National Trail stretches as far as Winchester.

In 1990, the South Downs Campaign was launched by a coalition of pressure groups representing local, regional and national organisations to fight for National Park recognition. Several million visitors to the Downs each year could not be wrong. Could they?

Twenty years later, after lengthy Inquiries and Appeals, and more than 60 years after the Hobhouse Report to the post-war government of Clement Attlee included the Downs in a list of 12 proposed National Parks for England and Wales, Environment Secretary Hilary Benn finally

The SDW traces the length of the Downs from Eastbourne to Winchester

gave the go-ahead. The South Downs would become the 10th National Park south of the border, in 2011.

PLANTS AND WILDLIFE OF THE DOWNS

The flowers appear on the earth; the time of the singing of birds is come

Song of Solomon

What makes the South Downs so special?

Since beauty is in the eye of the beholder, everyone drawn to the National Park will have their own response to its lure. It could be a sense of space that attracts, or the subtle curves and folds of the landscape, the steeply plunging north-facing slopes, the dazzling white cliffs at the eastern end, the intimate inner valleys. It could be its history, or its villages. For the walker with an eye for more than just a view with a footpath disappearing through it, a good part of its appeal must surely rest on the flowers that speckle the downland and the birdsong that serenades each mile.

The thin soil of the downland, lying on an immense bed of chalk, is sorely deficient in certain minerals, yet a variety of plant species will be in flower from spring right through to autumn. Among those that favour chalk-rich soils are the rough hawkbit, common milkwort, bulbous buttercup and salad burnet. On open grasslands, the regular grazing by sheep and rabbits over hundreds of years has kept the natural spread of scrub and woodland in check, which has enabled flowering plants to thrive, but elsewhere isolated deposits of clay-with-flint indicate the existence of deeper, more fertile soils that encourage small clumps of trees to stand out in an otherwise bare and open land.

The South Downs is a natural habitat for many different orchids

Cowslips are an unofficial symbol of the Downs

In West Sussex and the Hampshire Downs beechwood 'hangers' characterise the steep flanks and continue onto the escarpment. But the beech is not the only tree to flourish here, for oak, ash and yew are also common – the ancient yews at Kingley Vale, northwest of Chichester, are thought to be among Britain's oldest living plants and are well worth a visit.

In springtime the cowslip (*Primula veris*) makes its appearance on open downland, and on a few select slopes overlooking the Weald it spreads a great carpet of yellow in April and May. Almost ubiquitous on the South Downs, with some justification the cowslip could be taken as its symbol, for the collection of lightly scented, tube-shaped flowers opening to a cupped 'face' are among the natural gems of the National Park – a single

stem can host literally dozens of individual flower heads.

At the same time the common bluebell (*Hyacinthoides nonscripta*) drifts across steep banks where there's ample shade, and fills acres of broadleaved woodland with its brilliant colouring, sometimes interspersed with greater stitchwort (*Stellaria holostea*) or red campion (*Silene dioica*). In those same woodlands, wood sorrel (*Oxalis acetosella*) also comes into flower in April and May.

In spring and early summer a number of different orchids appear: the early purple, common spotted, and the scented fragrant orchid among them.

Spiky bushes of gorse (*Ules europaeus*), the yellow kidney vetch (*Anthyllis vulneraria*) and horseshoe vetch (*Hippocrepis comosa*) are all members of the pea family and are common to chalky soil, the last two flowering from May to August, while gorse flowers golden almost year-round. On rough grasslands and sunny woodland margins, marjoram (*Origanum vulgare*) is mainly a summer-flowering plant whose leaves, when crushed, smell of mint. Also seen throughout the South Downs on the chalk grassland, the small scabious (*Scabiosa columbaria*) flowers from July to September.

But the prize for the most eye-catching and colourful display must surely go to the common poppy (*Papaver rhoeas*), which invades grassland and arable field alike. It's not unusual on a summer's day to gaze across a broad view where swathes of brilliant red or scarlet reach into the distance. Draw closer and you may find long-stemmed chicory (*Cichorium intybus*) growing amidst the poppies, their beautiful pale-blue flower heads appearing delicate by contrast with their more powerful neighbours.

Poppies, seen almost everywhere on the South Downs in summer

Writing about the South Downs in 1893, the Victorian essayist Richard Jefferies commented: 'Under the September sun, flowers may still be found in sheltered places, as at the side of furze [gorse], on the highest of the Downs. Wild thyme continues to bloom – the shepherd's thyme – wild mignonette, blue scabious, white dropwort, yellow bedstraw, and the large purple blooms of greater knapweed. Grasshoppers hop among the short dry grass; bees and humblebees are buzzing about, and … the furze is everywhere full of finches' (*Nature Near London*).

Finches, yes, gathering in flocks in autumn and winter; brambling and chaffinch, thrush and warbler swarm over areas of scrub, attracted by the insect life that scrub supports. Redwing and fieldfare are common migrants, returning to the Downs in the autumn from their breeding grounds in northern Europe. The wheatear is a summer visitor, scavenging on the ground in search of insects. Ground nesting birds such as the meadow pipit and corn bunting are downland favourites, as is the lapwing (or peewit) which lays its eggs among open plough tracings.

But it is the skylark that will suddenly rise from the ground trilling its mellifluous song, then hovers as a tiny speck, singing all the while. No song could better conjour a landscape than this; it is the unmistakable soundtrack to the South Downs.

Typical butterflies, such as the adonis blue, chalkhill blue and common blue all feed on chalkland plants like the horseshoe vetch, while the marbled white is attracted to thistles on rough grassland.

Animal life ranges from tiny spiders and grasshoppers to roe and

Used by the SDW, this track carries the walk beyond the Clayton windmills (Walk 15)

fallow deer. Rabbits and hares graze the open grasslands; badgers, being nocturnal creatures, usually emerge from their setts in the evening to feed, while foxes can be quite brazen in their daylight journeys.

WALKING ON THE DOWNS

Discover some excuse to be up there ... and, if not, go without any pretext. Lands of gold have been found, and lands of spices and precious merchandise; but this is the land of health.

Richard Jefferies
(1848–1887)

The very best of the Downs can only be enjoyed on foot, and the 40 walks described in this guide have been chosen to serve as an introduction to some of the finest countryside in southern England. Stretching throughout the National Park, each of the routes is circular, beginning and ending at the same place; wherever possible, these places can be accessed by public transport.

No walk is more than 11 miles/17.5km long – the shortest is just under 5 miles/8km – but there's as much enjoyment to be had in a ramble of modest length, as may be found in a march that covers 20 miles or more. Size and distance have no meaning here: it's what you experience as you wander, and what you remember afterwards, that count.

Enthusiasts know full well that walking should not be confined to the summer months, for every season has its own unique brand of beauty, its own rewards, and a frosty winter's day can hold as much magic for the walker as any in balmy July. Nature serves each season well: spring's vibrant eruption of flowers and jubilant birdsong; summer's warmth and long hours of daylight encouraging full growth in field, meadow and woodland; autumn's touch of Midas, its mists, migrations and mushrooms; and winter's stark outlines of naked trees, long shadows and harsh frosts.

As someone once remarked, there's no such thing as bad weather when you're properly dressed. But being properly dressed will make all the difference to one's enjoyment of a day spent wandering the Downs.

Choose clothing suitable for the season; clothing that is sufficiently adaptable to accommodate the vagaries of our climate. Footwear needs to be comfortable: if it is you'll feel almost as fresh at the end of the day, as when you set out at the start. For summer walks, shorts may be adequate on the majority of footpaths described in this book, but bear in mind that brambles and nettles often stray across infrequently used paths. An inexpensive pair of overtrousers (preferably with a zipped ankle-gusset so they can be pulled on or off without removing walking boots) will prove useful. A lightweight collapsible umbrella can be worth carrying for protection from a sudden shower. Since much of the region covered by

The escarpment near Devil's Dyke (Walk 16) makes a popular launch site for paragliders

this guide is open high ground, windy days can seem much colder than they really are, so remember to carry some warm, windproof clothing.

Carry a few plasters in case of blisters or the odd scratch; take a flask of liquid refreshment, and something to nibble should energy wane. An Ordnance Survey map will be needed in the unlikely event of your getting lost. It will also present you with a broader picture of the countryside through which your walk leads than may be gained from the OS extracts included within these pages. Details of the specific map sheets required are provided at the head of each walk described. I've also noted the availability of refreshments, where they occur. Most of these are to be found at country pubs, although I stress that I have no personal experience of the majority of those mentioned, so no endorsement is intended (I'd sooner chew on an apple while enjoying an open view than sit in a pub!). There has also been a spate of pub closures in recent years, so be warned that you may find the one you'd planned to visit is no longer open. If this is the case, a note to me via the publisher (address given at the front of the book) would be welcome, and I'll ensure a correction is made in the next edition of this guide.

Should you plan to stop at a pub or café during your walk, please be considerate if your footwear is muddy and either leave your boots in the porch, or cover them with plastic bags.

It is assumed that anyone out for a walk in the countryside will have a love for that countryside, and treat it with respect. Sadly, evidence contradicts that assumption, for litter is still found where only walkers go. So I make a plea that all who go walking in the South Downs National Park will be careful not to leave litter, and help make the Downs even more attractive for all by removing any you find. A plastic bag is useful for carrying rubbish away – keep one in your rucksack for this purpose.

It has taken millions of years of evolution to create the South Downs. It has taken thousands of years for Man

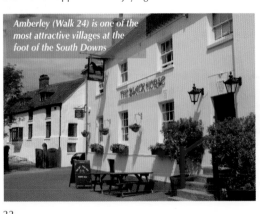

Amberley (Walk 24) is one of the most attractive villages at the foot of the South Downs

to mould it into the living landscape we cherish today, and more than 60 years to establish it as a National Park. Let each of us treat it with the love and respect it deserves.

USING THE GUIDE

Maps

This guide contains sections of the Ordnance Survey map relevant to each walk described, and are taken from the 1:50,000 series which it is hoped will be sufficient at 1¼ inches to the mile (2cm = 1km) to provide an overview and a general outline of the route to be walked. However, for greater detail and a wider perspective the Explorer series drawn at a scale of 1:25,000 (2½ inches to 1 mile; or 4cm = 1km) is recommended, with the individual sheet information given at the head of each walk description. Most of these Explorer sheets cover several walks.

Grid references are frequently quoted to enable you to locate a given position on the map. Each OS sheet is divided by a series of vertical and horizontal lines to create a grid. These lines are individually numbered, and these numbers are quoted at the top, bottom, and sides of each sheet. Numbers increase from left to right for vertical lines (known as 'eastings'), and from top to bottom for horizontal lines ('northings').

Each grid forms part of a much larger 100,000m square identified by a unique two-letter code. These letters

are printed within the section headed The National Grid Reference System found in the key to each sheet, and are quoted in this guide immediately before the six-figure grid reference.

To identify an exact position on the map from a given grid reference, take the first two digits from the six-figure number quoted. These refer to the 'eastings' line on the OS map. The third digit is estimated in tenths of the square moving eastwards from that line. Next, take the fourth and fifth digits referring to the 'northings' line, and then the final digit estimating the number of tenths of the square reading up the sheet. Using this grid reference you should be able to pin-point the exact position referred to in the text.

Times and Distances

Distances quoted in the text have been measured on the individual OS maps and double-checked using a pedometer, so they should be reasonably accurate. Please note that heights quoted on OS maps are in metres, not feet, and grid lines are spaced at intervals of 1km.

Allow 2–2½ miles per hour for your walk, without prolonged stops. Reckon on walking a little slower after rain when conditions may be heavy or a little greasy underfoot. When accompanied by children or inexperienced walkers – or indeed, when walking in a group – allow extra time, especially if there are stiles to cross.

Leaving the route of the South Downs Way, this stile takes the walker onto Salt Hill (Walk 34)

PUBLIC TRANSPORT AND CAR PARKING

Several railway companies operate lines that run in the vicinity of the South Downs National Park, and where specific walks may be accessed by train, a note of the nearest station is given. The same goes

PUBLIC TRANSPORT INFORMATION

Southern Railways operate services from London Victoria to Brighton, Chichester, Eastbourne, Lewes, and Portsmouth

South West Trains operate services from London to Brighton and Portsmouth

First Capital Connect operate between Brighton and Bedford

First Greater Western have a twice daily service between Brighton and Cardiff

National Rail Enquiries ☎ 08457 484950 (24 hour service) www.nationalrail.co.uk

Traveline Bus Service ☎ 0870 608 2608 www.traveline.org.uk

National Express Coaches ☎ 08705 808080 www.nationalexpress.co.uk

See also www.infotransport.co.uk or www.buses.co.uk

The dedicated South Downs website www.visitsouthdowns.com also provides valuable public transport information.

for bus services, but it would not be practical to give details of times – or even the frequency of services (bus or train) – since these are likely to change during the period this guidebook is in print.

The location, including grid reference, of a suitable car park is included at the beginning of each walk should you use your own transport to reach the start of a walk. However, where there is no official parking facility available, please park sensibly and with consideration for local residents and farm vehicles, making sure you do not cause an obstruction. If you park near a church, please avoid service times. Do not leave valuables in your vehicle, and be sure to lock it before setting out on your walk.

WHERE TO STAY

A wide range of accommodation is available throughout the South Downs National Park, ranging from a handful of campsites, YHA hostels, camping barns and independent hostels, to privately owned B&Bs, pubs with rooms, and a variety of hotels. The South Downs website www. visitsouthdowns.com provides details and is recommended. For more specific information about youth hostels, their location and facilities, please see Appendix A for the address of the YHA national office. Camping barns and independent hostels that cater for groups,

families and individuals, are listed in the Handbook of Independent Hostels UK published by The Backpackers Press, or go to www.independent hostelguide.co.uk.

THE COUNTRY CODE

1. Enjoy the countryside and respect its life and work
2. Guard against all risk of fire
3. Fasten all gates
4. Keep dogs under close control
5. Keep to public paths across farmland
6. Use gates and stiles to cross fences, hedges and walls
7. Leave livestock, crops and machinery alone
8. Take litter home
9. Help to keep all water clean
10. Protect wildlife, plants and trees
11. Take special care on country roads
12. Make no unnecessary noise.

It was Octavia Hill, that indefatigable Victorian champion of the countryside and a co-founder of the National Trust, whose words sum up the spirit of the Country Code:

'Let the grass growing for hay be respected, let the primrose roots be left in their loveliness in the hedges, the birds unmolested and the gates shut. If those who frequented country places would consider those who live there, they would better deserve, and more often retain, the rights and privileges they enjoy.'

The very substance of the Downs is revealed in the chalk cliffs of the Seven Sisters (Walk 5)

THE SOUTH DOWNS ON THE WEB

For details of how to get there, public transport, accommodation and other tourist information relevant to the area, visit www.visitsouthdowns.com.

WALK 1

Eastbourne to Birling Gap and East Dean

Distance	9½ miles (15km)
Map	OS Explorer 123 Eastbourne & Beachy Head 1:25,000
Start	Dukes Drive, Eastbourne (TV 600 972)
Access	By local bus. Dukes Drive is on B2103
Parking	Streetside parking nearby
Refreshments	Refreshment kiosk at start of walk, café at Birling Gap, pub and café in East Dean

A scenic, but quite strenuous, circular walk with some steep ascents and descents. The first half, as far as Birling Gap, is mostly clifftop walking overlooking the sea, while the second half explores downland ridges and valleys inland. Beachy Head, that icon of the Sussex coast, is a major feature in the early stages, and there's an opportunity to make a diversion onto the foreshore to view it from below.

The walk begins at the start of the South Downs Way, where Dukes Drive makes a sharp bend near St Bede's School at Eastbourne's southernmost point. While the SDW actually climbs steeply up the downland slope, we take a path to the left, signed to Whitbread Hole and Cow Gap. It goes along the side of a refreshment kiosk, rises steadily then curves to the right before sloping down towards Whitbread Hole, an impressive amphitheatre (a 'dry valley') in which there's a sports field.

Keeping to the seaward side of Whitbread Hole go ahead through a gap in a hedgeline, and soon come to a brief flight of descending steps at the bottom of which the path forks. Unless you plan to divert to **Cow Gap** and the foreshore for a dramatic view of Beachy Head, take the right branch.

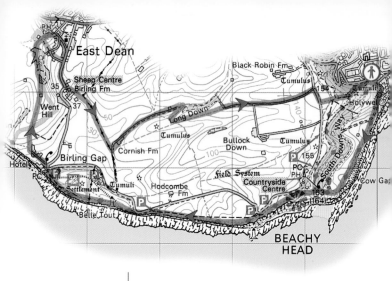

East Dean

The towering cliff of Beachy Head, seen from the shoreline diversion

Cow Gap gives access to the foreshore by way of a steep wooden ladder. At the bottom of this pick your way among rocks heading to the right (beware rockfall and incoming tides) below ever-steepening chalk cliffs,

until turning a corner you gain a tremendous view of Beachy Head soaring 536ft (163m) above the surf, with the red-and-white-ringed lighthouse dwarfed below it – a there-and-back diversion from the main walk of about 1 mile (1.5km).

Beyond the Cow Gap fork the path continues along cropped grass on the lower cliffs before curving sharply to the right (west) and rising very steeply. At the head of the slope join the route of the South Downs Way which crosses a tarmac path making a loop to a vantage point, then curves along the clifftop to **Beachy Head**.

From here to Birling Gap the walk follows the route of the South Downs Way along the clifftops. Do not stray too close to the edge as the cliffs are prone to crumbling. This is a walk of great scenic beauty: sea to one side, rolling downland spreading away on the other, while ahead the white-edged cliffs lead the eye towards Seaford Head. With its cropped thatch of grass and dramatic white cliffs, this forms part of a treasured Heritage Coast.

In 1999 a massive **rockfall** destroyed a section of Beachy Head's cliff-face, a potent reminder of its vulnerability. Heeding the warning, the owners of the disused Belle Tout lighthouse (built in 1831 but made redundant in 1901) physically moved it a short distance down the slope, away from the cliff edge. The cottages at Birling Gap are also succumbing, one by one, to cliff-edge erosion.

The way slopes down almost to road level below the stumpy former lighthouse of **Belle Tout** (now a private dwelling), where you come onto a tarmac path rising to it. Pass round the inland side of the boundary wall, then resume across the clifftop to **Birling Gap** at TV 554 960. Refreshments may be had here.

Cross the car park and take a stony track beyond the public toilet block and pass a few houses. The way forks by the last house, with the South Downs Way cutting left to Exceat. Leaving that route now, go ahead on a bridleway signed to East Dean. Rising up a slope among gorse bushes, a bridle gate gives access to the NT-owned estate of Crowlink. Through a second gate follow a grass track onto the crest of **Went Hill** where you'll see an orange-roofed barn. Ignore the track which now curves left, and keep ahead on the crest of the hill to enter a wooded area. On coming to a flint wall follow this to the left to reach a kissing gate. Through this maintain direction alongside a fence and shortly come to a stile. Over the stile aim slightly right ahead through a narrowing section of meadow enclosed by bushes and trees, to where a fence and flintstone wall meet. The wall is crossed by two stone stiles which give options for the continuing walk.

Shorter walk
This avoids East Dean and the opportunity for refreshment, crosses the right-hand stile, then follows a path angling down and across a grass slope to reach the head of a track. Follow this to the left, alongside a playing field to join the Birling Gap Road at TV 556 974.

The main walk crosses the stile directly ahead, wanders down the slope, then veers left through trees. Emerging from the trees bear sharply to the right to a field gate giving onto a drive, which brings you into the lovely flint-walled village of **East Dean**. Veer right and in a few paces you'll come to the village green with the Tiger Inn on its far side. The road forks. Take the lower branch signed to Birling Gap: this leads past a little church and on to a T-junction. Turn right along Birling Gap Road to reach the playing field at TV 556 974.

The two routes having rejoined, keep alongside the road until it curves right by the **Seven Sisters Sheep Centre**. Walk ahead along a drive towards Birling Manor, then through a gate on the left. Pass to the left of a house, then through a second gate to walk along the left-hand

side of a woodland shaw. Come to another gate at the end of a flintstone wall and take the right-hand option on a path signed to Belle Tout.

Family strollers wander down to Birling Gap, with the Seven Sisters ahead

When you draw level with **Cornish Farm** (TV 564 964) turn left in the direction of Warren Hill. Pass along the left-hand side of the farm and its out-buildings, then through a gate keep ahead along a track that leads into a valley known as Wigden's Bottom. Come to a water treatment building, shown as a pump-ing station on the 1:25,000 map, and keep ahead a short distance beyond it as far as a dew pond seen on the left. Now turn sharply to the right at a junction, and angle up the slope (virtually cutting back) on a bridleway signed to Beachy Head.

Passing through a line of scrub come onto Long Down and bear left. Remain along the crest of the Downs – a big and spacious landscape grazed by innumerable sheep – roughly following the right-hand fenceline that leads to a bridle gate with a view of Bullockdown Farm off to the right. The way becomes enclosed by fences and

Low-growing mallow is common on the clifftops

a flintstone wall, and eventually brings you to a road at TV 591 971. Eastbourne is now seen ahead.

Turn right alongside the road as far as a flint wall, then cross the road with care to follow a faint grass path ahead alongside gorse bushes. At a crossing grass path maintain direction down the slope. When this path forks, take the right branch ahead, now on the South Downs Way once more, and descend steeply to the refreshment kiosk on Dukes Drive where the walk began.

WALK 2

Butts Brow to Jevington and Friston

Distance	7 miles (11km)
Map	OS Explorer 123 Eastbourne & Beachy Head 1:25,000
Start	Butts Brow car park, Willingdon (TQ 580 017)
Access	Via Butts Lane, Willingdon
Parking	At Butts Brow (fee payable)
Refreshments	Pub and tearooms at Jevington

At the easternmost end of the South Downs, Butts Brow overlooks the narrow dry valley of Tas Combe which falls away to Willingdon on the outskirts of Eastbourne. From Butts Brow itself, and from neighbouring Combe Hill, an immense panorama reaches far out across the Weald in one direction, over the low-lying Pevensey Levels in another, and a succession of downland ridges elsewhere. This walk is a delight of big open views, neat valleys and forest rides, in which the true nature of the South Downs is revealed within the first few minutes.

Leave the car park by a kissing gate and follow a footpath signed to Combe Hill and Wannock, walking parallel with the road up which you've just travelled. Off to the right the coastline can be seen curving towards Bexhill and Hastings. Before long come to a bench seat by a dome of scrub. A short distance beyond this veer left where the path forks, and rise onto **Combe Hill**, over which the way then slopes down between gorse bushes, and crosses a stile. Over a second stile maintain direction down a long sloping spur of downland. On coming to an oak post bearing a Wealdway waymark continue ahead for about 80m to a second oak post. Leave the Wealdway here and veer left into trees and scrub where the path then strikes through an 'avenue' of gorse, before coming to a kissing gate. Maintain direction across a sloping

33

field to a stile giving access to a woodland strip. Out of the trees descend to a white cottage beside which a gate leads onto a narrow lane that takes you into **Jevington**'s main street at TQ 563 014. For refreshments in Jevington turn right along the road to reach The Eight Bells pub, or turn left to the Jevington Tea Garden.

Turn left for a short distance, then bear right at the entrance to a small car park where a bridleway heads up the slope, initially between trees and bushes. On reaching the brow of the hill enter **Friston Forest** and walk ahead on a broad ride signed to West Dean. Very shortly come to a major crossing track. Continue ahead, ignoring alternative paths and tracks, for a little over ½ mile (800m) until you come to a four-way crossing, which is marked by an oak

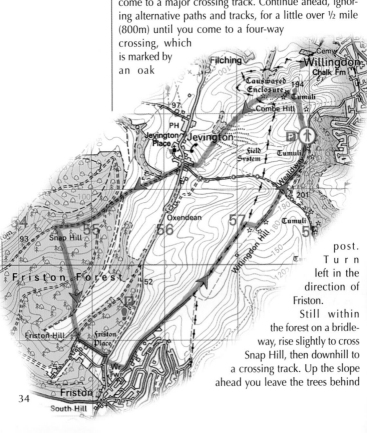

post. Turn left in the direction of Friston.

Still within the forest on a bridleway, rise slightly to cross Snap Hill, then downhill to a crossing track. Up the slope ahead you leave the trees behind

The chalk-loving wild clematis in flower

on gaining Friston Hill, with its broad open views and a racehorse training area. Take care when crossing the ride immediately ahead, and maintain direction down the slope towards more forest clothing Butchershole Bottom. At the foot of the slope keep ahead alongside the grounds of **Friston Place**, and eventually come to the Jevington–Friston road at TV 552 988.

Directly ahead on the opposite side of the road go through a bridle gate and bear right. Walk parallel with the road to a line of trees opposite the entrance to Friston Place, then turn left along a shallow sunken bridle-way rising up the slope. Near the head of the slope go through another bridle gate and turn left along the narrow Willingdon Road on the edge of Friston.

Passing several fine properties that enjoy huge vistas, when the road ends continue ahead on a hedge-lined track known as Friston Dencher. ▶ The track is a bridleway which leads to a gateway near Willingdon Hill. Go through the gateway and curve to the right onto **Willingdon Hill**, where the panorama becomes

There are splendid views every step of the way, including Jevington's church seen in the valley to the north.

even more extensive. To the south the former light-house of Belle Tout can be seen, as can Birling Gap and the clifftop of the Seven Sisters leading round to Seaford Head.

With flintstone ruins nearby turn left on a crossing track. Go through a gate where the way forks. Keep ahead on the left branch which remains on the track, and soon come to a second gate with a seat nearby overlooking Jevington. Through the gate cross a track used by the South Downs Way, and maintain direction, now following the route of the Wealdway which leads back to the car park on Butts Brow.

> **The Wealdway** is a long-distance walk of 82 miles (132km) which begins at Gravesend on the south bank of the Thames, and strikes southward across the North Downs and Greensand Ridge in Kent, then follows the River Medway into Tonbridge. Leaving Tonbridge it crosses several High Weald ridges into East Sussex, goes over Ashdown Forest and reaches the South Downs at Wilmington, before ending on the edge of Eastbourne.

*Jevington church,
where Walk 3 begins*

WALK 3

Jevington to Friston Forest and the Long Man

Distance	7½ miles (12km)
Map	OS Explorer 123 Eastbourne & Beachy Head 1:25,000
Start	St Andrew's Church, Jevington (TQ 562 015)
Access	By minor road between A27 (Polegate) and A259 (East Dean)
Parking	Either by Jevington church (avoid service times), or marked car park off Jevington High Street at TQ 563 014
Refreshments	Pub and tearooms in Jevington

The contrast of broadleaved woods and open downland adds to the diversity of this walk. There's also a nature reserve; a close view of Britain's tallest chalk figure; big panoramic views that take in the spreading Downs, the rich tartan-patterned Weald, and a long stretch of coast. There's a small hamlet and an attractive village, and the walk also links sections of the South Downs Way and the Wealdway. Take a packed lunch and something to drink, and make a day of it.

Begin the walk on the route taken by the South Downs Way where it passes along the left-hand side of the attractive church of St Andrew in **Jevington**. There's a small car park (please do not use during service times) at the start of the narrow, tree-lined bridleway which rises alongside a series of paddocks. The gradient steepens among mature horse chestnut trees shortly before you come to a signed four-way junction. Leave the SDW here and turn left on another bridleway angling gently across the wooded downland flank.

Jevington is said to be a one-time smugglers' haunt, and The Eight Bells pub was once owned by a renowned smuggler, James Pettit (known as Jevington Jigg) who was sentenced to serve 17 years in Botany

Bay. The lovely old church of St Andrew has a squat Saxon tower thought to date from around AD900–950. Today the village has close links with the world of horse racing.

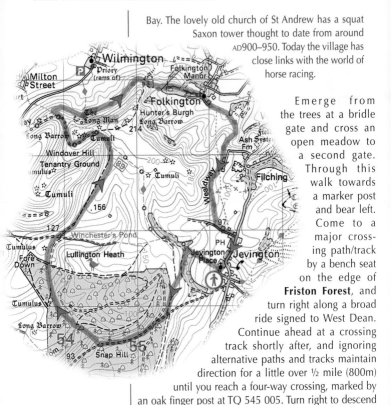

Emerge from the trees at a bridle gate and cross an open meadow to a second gate. Through this walk towards a marker post and bear left. Come to a major crossing path/track by a bench seat on the edge of **Friston Forest**, and turn right along a broad ride signed to West Dean. Continue ahead at a crossing track shortly after, and ignoring alternative paths and tracks maintain direction for a little over ½ mile (800m) until you reach a four-way crossing, marked by an oak finger post at TQ 545 005. Turn right to descend the slope on the route signed to the 'Long Man'.

Halfway down the slope the way forks. Continue directly ahead, and at the foot of the hill you'll reach a junction of tracks. Bear left, then almost immediately veer right on the continuing broad track to the Long Man. This rises gently between trees and scrub, and near the head of the slope enters **Lullington Heath Nature Reserve** where the way is flanked by gorse. ◀ Keep ahead to arrive at another junction of chalk and flint tracks, from where you gain a lovely view left to the westward continuation of the Downs, with Alfriston seen below in the Cuckmere

In springtime the blackthorn bushes are fluffed with blossom, the speckled hills rolling away to the right appearing even more attractive than usual.

valley. Go ahead to a second track which you then follow to the right. This soon curves left and takes you through a gateway into an open hilltop field. Across this you come to a bridle gate. Before going through this gate, pause to enjoy the backward view – an uplifting panorama that includes the coastline virtually from Beachy Head to Seaford Head; the large chalk outline of a white horse on the slopes of High and Over; Alfriston once more, with Bostal Hill above it; and projecting spurs of the South Downs stretching off to the west.

Looking back to Jevington from the tree-lined bridleway

Through the bridle gate follow the left-hand fenceline studded with gorse, and soon rejoin the South Downs Way where the route curves left above the dry valley of Deep Dean. Arrive at another bridle gate on Windover Hill. At this point you're directly above the head of the unseen Long Man of Wilmington, and if you walk forward a few paces from the path, you'll gain a dramatic view of Arlington Reservoir and the Weald stretching beyond Wilmington village.

The South Downs Way bears left, then curves right as it slopes down a sunken track. As you descend this and

39

veer left, a minor chalk path goes off ahead. Follow this, and descend through a steep and narrow gully. Halfway down the slope, with Milton Street seen in the valley below, come to a crossing path and turn right through another bridle gate. The path now curves along the flank of the Downs with glorious views ahead, and takes you directly below the **Long Man of Wilmington**.

THE LONG MAN OF WILMINGTON

The Long Man of Wilmington is said to be Britain's largest chalk figure. Set on the flank of Wilmington Hill he gazes north across the Weald, he is 226ft (69m) long, holding a 250ft (76m) stave in each hand. His origin is unknown, but speculation suggests he could have been created in the Bronze Age, about 4000 years ago; or perhaps he was a product of the Saxons. Who knows? But whoever was responsible for this most famous of downland chalk figures, he was so cleverly created that from whichever angle he is viewed, he is never seriously foreshortened, despite the steepness of the hill.

Beech gives way to sycamore, ash and horse chestnut, and masses of wild garlic in springtime.

At the foot of the Long Man there's a concrete dew pond, and a gate taking a path between fields to Wilmington village. Ignore this and continue ahead, now on the route of the Wealdway. Eventually go through yet another gate to join a more prominent track (muddy after prolonged rain) which eases along the lower edge of beechwoods. ◄

Come to the head of a narrow road by the secluded 13th-century church of St Peter, **Folkington**, at TQ 559 038. Here you veer slightly right on a broad stony track which continues along the right-hand side of the vegetated wall surrounding the churchyard, taking the walk on the final 1½ mile (3.5km) stretch to Jevington. With the steep slope of Folkington Hill to the right, the track eventually narrows between trees and scrub. On coming to a crossing track, veer left and soon arrive at the northern end of Jevington's main street opposite The Old Post Office. Turn right, and shortly after passing The Eight Bells pub, follow the footpath which rises slightly above the right-hand side of the road and brings you into the churchyard of St Andrew's.

WALK 4

Jevington to Alfriston and Wilmington

Distance	8½ miles (13.5km)
Map	OS Explorer 123 Eastbourne & Beachy Head 1:25,000
Start	St Andrew's Church, Jevington (TQ 562 015)
Access	By minor road between A27 (Polegate) and A259 (East Dean)
Parking	By Jevington church (avoid service times), or marked car park off Jevington High Street at TQ 563 014
Refreshments	Pub and tearooms in Jevington, pubs, cafés and shops in Alfriston, pubs in Milton Street and Wilmington

A slightly longer variation of Walk 3, this route crosses the Downs between Jevington and Alfriston along the South Downs Way, then follows the Cuckmere for a short distance before crossing fields to Wilmington with fine views of the Long Man, and returning to Jevington via the bridleway which passes Folkington church.

With the church of St Andrew to your right, follow the fenced bridleway of the South Downs Way alongside paddocks, then rise into woodland, where you come to a four-way junction of paths. Maintain direction until emerging from the woods near the head of the slope, where the path forks. Turn right here, and after a few paces go through a bridle gate. Before long, as the path takes you onto the open Downs, a view to the right reveals the Pevensey Levels beyond Polegate.

Eventually the way curves left round the head of the deep combe of Deep Dene and goes through a gate. Continue round to the left to pass just below the summit of Windover Hill, on which there's the remains of a long barrow. If you stray onto that mound a magnificent panoramic view opens before you. Losing height now, pass the flat-topped site of Windover Reservoir and continue

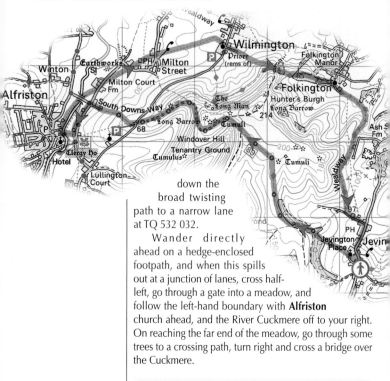

down the broad twisting path to a narrow lane at TQ 532 032.

Wander directly ahead on a hedge-enclosed footpath, and when this spills out at a junction of lanes, cross half-left, go through a gate into a meadow, and follow the left-hand boundary with **Alfriston** church ahead, and the River Cuckmere off to your right. On reaching the far end of the meadow, go through some trees to a crossing path, turn right and cross a bridge over the Cuckmere.

> For refreshments keep ahead to **Alfriston** High Street where there are shops, pubs and cafés.

For the continuing walk turn right on the west side of the river, and follow a raised footpath along the riverbank as far as a brick-built road bridge known as Long Bridge. Here you cross to the east bank and go through a kissing gate on the left. A footpath now takes you across two link-ing fields to a minor road near **Milton Court Farm**. Turn left, and after about 200 yards cross a stile on the right. Bear left for a few paces into an adjoining open field, then

take the footpath which cuts across it. On the far side cross the minor road again, and maintain direction through the next field to a gate located to the right of a Dutch barn.

From Windover Hill above The Long Man, Wilmington can be seen in the flat land below

In a few paces come to a path junction and continue half-right ahead, aiming for the right-hand end of farm buildings, where you come onto the road once again in **Milton Street** at TQ 535 041. (There's a pub a short distance to the right.) Cross the road, and over a stile follow a footpath cutting across a large sloping field, with the spire of Wilmington church seen at the head of the slope. On the way across the field the **Long Man of Wilmington** comes into view (see the note about the Long Man in Walk 3 above).

The path leads directly to **Wilmington** churchyard. Wander through the churchyard and out to the village street. ▶ The continuing walk crosses the road and goes up a track used as a bridleway. Rising up a slope you come to a section of beechwood where the angle eases to skirt a hill before coming to a track by St Peter's Church, **Folkington**, at TQ 559 038.

For pub refreshments walk left for about 500 yards.

43

Alfriston peeps through the trees across Cuckmere water meadows

The 13th-century **St Peter's Church** in Folkington has a squat shingle spire projecting from a flint-walled tower. Inside there are box pews, and among the memorials, there's one to Viscount Monckton, an advisor to Edward VIII in the days leading to the king's abdication.

Veer slightly right onto the gravel track which takes you past the church and along the foot of Folkington Hill. After a while the track narrows and is enclosed by hedges tangled with wild clematis or old man's beard. Ignore alternative paths to right and left and eventually, shortly before reaching Jevington, you come to a crossing track. Bear left and soon pass between houses to reach the main street in Jevington, opposite The Old Post Office. Turn right, wander past the Eight Bells pub, and when the footpath rises above the road and curves to the right, enter the churchyard through a swivel gate to arrive at St Andrew's church where the walk began.

The Cuckmere Community Bus is a boon for Alfriston-based walkers

WALK 5

Exceat to East Dean and the Seven Sisters

Distance	8 miles (12.5km)
Map	OS Explorer 123 Eastbourne & Beachy Head 1:25,000
Start	Seven Sisters Country Park Visitor Centre, Exceat (TV 519 995)
Access	By bus from Eastbourne, Seaford or Brighton; the Visitor Centre is on the A259
Parking	Pay and display car park in woodland behind the Visitor Centre
Refreshments	Café at the Visitor Centre, pub and café in East Dean, café at Birling Gap

The coastline between Beachy Head and Cuckmere Haven is without question one of the finest in the British Isles. The eastern half of the clifftop was included in Walk 1, but the western half forms the visual and physical highlight of this current walk. It is a tremendous route with a variety of interests, not least the Seven Sisters section. The two small villages of Westdean and East Dean have numerous charming cottages and houses; the churches of both villages are matched for interest by that of Friston; there's Friston Forest, a glimpse of Friston Place, the cropped downland of Went Hill with its great arcing view of the sea, and, at the end of the Seven Sisters roller-coaster, a fine view onto Cuckmere Haven and the Cuckmere Valley reaching inland to the north.

At the junction of Litlington Road and the A259 a few paces west of the Living World and Visitor Centre at Exceat, a path is signed to Westdean. Passing through the lower section of a wooded car park, the bridleway increases in size as it cuts through Friston Forest, initially heading north but then curving roughly eastward before emerging alongside a pond on the edge of **Westdean**. Turn left in front of Pond Cottage, then right along a narrow road (sign to Friston 2 miles). This leads through the tiny village,

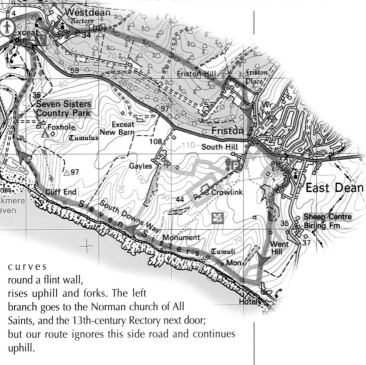

curves
round a flint wall,
rises uphill and forks. The left
branch goes to the Norman church of All
Saints, and the 13th-century Rectory next door;
but our route ignores this side road and continues
uphill.

> **Westdean** is a very small but attractive village at the
> end of a cul-de-sac almost completely surrounded by
> Friston Forest. It is said that the Saxon King Alfred had
> an estate here, but there's no sign of the palace he is
> supposed to have built in the village in AD850, although
> there is conjecture that the site may lie beneath the
> ruins of a medieval manor house. During Alfred's reign
> the Cuckmere estuary was much more extensive than
> it is today (it was then known simply as Dene) and it is
> thought he maintained a fleet here.

The Forestry Commission road leads directly up to the
main part of **Friston Forest**, then becomes a stony track
signed to Jevington and Friston. Keep along this until,

47

shortly after passing a lone house on the left, the track forks. Take the right branch, a broad bare-earth bridleway striking uphill (the left fork goes to Jevington). Lined in summer by a scarlet 'avenue' of rosebay willowherb, the track gives easy walking, then slopes downhill and curves to the left. Leave it at this point and walk straight ahead to climb among more trees until you come to the large meadowland of **Friston Hill** with a water tower seen on the wooded skyline ahead.

Managed by the Forestry Commission, **Friston Forest** consists of almost 2000 acres of mixed woodland, with broad rides and several footpaths. Originally the forest was almost entirely deciduous, and during the 15th century it sheltered remnants of Jack Cade's peasant army.

Maintain direction along the right-hand edge of the meadow, then descend to a narrow lane by the entrance to **Friston Place** at TV 546 988. Turn left and follow the lane as it bends sharply to the right, and about 300 yards after the bend take an unmarked footpath on the right which goes through a gate in a wall surrounding parkland. Walk directly across to a kissing gate on the far side. A few steps take you onto the drive leading to Friston Place, across which you enter a sloping meadow and make for its top right-hand corner. A stile then takes the footpath into woodland and out to a junction of roads opposite a pond and church at **Friston** (TV 551 983).

Friston spills into the Downs and almost swamps its more attractive neighbour, East Dean. The little church of St Mary the Virgin stands on the western edge, and dates from the 11th century, while Friston Place, seen on the approach to the village, was built in about 1650. Until 1926, when it was blown down in a storm, a windmill stood in a field near the church.

Cross the A259 with care, enter the churchyard through a tapsell gate and, passing the lovely old

The Tiger Inn overlooks the village green at East Dean

church on your left, go out by another gate to a sloping meadow with a glimpse of the sea. At the bottom of the meadow you come into East Dean by the village hall. Bear right along a residential street, soon passing the village green on your left, beside which stands The Tiger Inn. The street forks: branch right (the upper option) along Went Way, at the end of which go through a field gate into a meadow and curve left, then rise along the lower edge of woodland. The path now makes a steady climb through the woods before emerging on the open downland of Went Hill.

Wander ahead to pass along the right-hand side of an orange-roofed barn, with a beautiful and far-reaching view across the Seven Sisters and towards Beachy Head, with the squat, disused Belle Tout lighthouse a prominent feature on the cliffs southeast of Birling Gap. The grass path takes you down to a gate near the white weatherboarded Seven Sisters Cottage. A few paces after this turn right onto the path of the South Downs Way which goes through another gate to begin the crossing of the Seven Sisters.

Note

Should you need refreshments, **do not** go through this second gate, but follow the alternative path which very soon brings you to the group of buildings at Birling Gap where there is a café.

Crossing the **Seven Sisters** is a glorious, often breezy walk, with magnificent views throughout. There are, in fact, eight 'sisters' – Went Hill Brow, Baily's Hill, Flat Hill, Flagstaff Brow, Brass Point, Rough Brow, Short Brow and Haven Brow – separated by steep-sided dry valleys known as 'bottoms' formed by ancient rivers at a time when the chalk cliffs extended much further seaward than they are now, but were then cut off when the tides pummelled and pounded the chalk away – a process that continues to this day.

The Cuckmere River near Exceat

Crossing the final 'sister', Haven Brow (so-named because it looks down onto the estuary of Cuckmere

Haven), the path of the South Downs Way veers right, but we continue ahead down the slope to cross a stile, then curve right and angle down to a kissing gate. The path continues to descend easily, passing a pillbox and through a gate brings you onto the valley path which leads all the way back to Exceat and the Seven Sisters Country Park Visitor Centre.

The Seven Sisters Country Park covers a large area of chalk downland east of Cuckmere Haven

Established by East Sussex County Council in 1971, and now managed by the South Downs Joint Committee, the **Seven Sisters Country Park** covers 690 acres (280 hectares) of chalk cliffs and downland spreading east of Cuckmere Haven. It is heavily used by walkers, for whom the route across the Seven Sisters from Birling Gap is a noted classic. The visitor centre is housed in a converted 18th-century barn, while midway between Exceat and Cuckmere Haven the Country Park has a campsite and camping barn in Foxhole Bottom. Visit **www.sevensisters.org.uk**.

WALK 6

Exceat to the Cuckmere Valley and Alfriston

Distance	7 miles (11km)
Map	OS Explorer 123 Eastbourne & Beachy Head 1:25,000
Start	Seven Sisters Country Park Visitor Centre, Exceat (TV 519995)
Access	By bus from Eastbourne, Seaford or Brighton; the Visitor Centre is on the A259
Parking	Pay and display car park in woodland behind the Visitor Centre
Refreshments	Pubs, cafés and restaurants at Exceat, Litlington and Alfriston.

South of Berwick the Cuckmere River has cut a slice through the South Downs. Once a major waterway, today the Cuckmere is a meagre stream which only grows in size and character between Alfriston and its estuary at Cuckmere Haven. Writhing among water meadows the river has footpaths on both east and west banks, and this circular walk uses sections of both. It begins by following the South Downs Way northward over the western limits of Friston Forest, then drops down to Litlington to join the Cuckmere into Alfriston, before returning to Exceat by way of the west bank footpath. An undemanding but very rewarding walk, there should be plenty of opportunities to study wildlife on the way.

A signpost on the Eastbourne side of the Visitor Centre beside the A259 directs the South Downs Way to Alfriston along a brief tarmac path between buildings, then through a kissing gate and up a downland slope. At the top of this slope you gain a lovely view south over the Cuckmere's valley to the sea beyond. A stone stile takes you over a wall and into **Friston Forest**, where you then descend a series of wood-braced steps, emerging at the foot of the slope in the hamlet of **Westdean**.

Continue ahead along a narrow road which becomes a track (at first a driveway to The Glebe) rising to another section of the forest. On coming to an upper garden boundary, turn left. When the track forks within Friston Forest keep ahead. At the end of a long open 'corridor' you come to a five-way junction and continue ahead, still following the acorn symbol of the South Downs Way. Descend on a narrow footpath between fences, then curve left at the foot of the slope alongside the boundary of **Charleston Manor**.

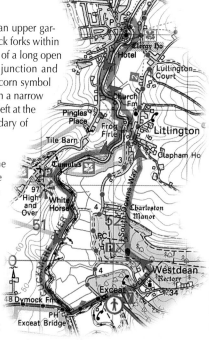

Charleston Manor is named in the Domesday Book as being in the hands of William the Conqueror's cup-bearer, Cerlestone. In the grounds can be seen a large, beautifully restored tithe barn, said to be 177ft (54m) long. The gardens are open to the public on set days in summer.

Keep alert for a stile on the right taking you away from the main path round Charleston Manor, and walk

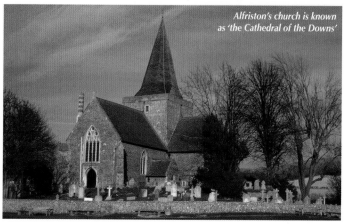

Alfriston's church is known as 'the Cathedral of the Downs'

53

up the left-hand edge of a sloping field and into a second field. At the end of this keep ahead, cross a stile and maintain direction with Alfriston church seen some way ahead. Through a kissing gate descend a steep grass slope into **Litlington**.

> **Litlington** is a picturesque, one-time smugglers' village of flint-walled cottages, a Norman church, and The Plough and Harrow pub. From the village, and from the footpath above it, a white horse may be seen carved on the slopes of High and Over on the west side of the valley. The return walk will pass directly below it.

Turn right along the main street, but a few paces beyond The Plough and Harrow turn left on a narrow enclosed footpath. Turn right when it forks, to wander upstream alongside the Cuckmere for about a mile (1.5km). Cross the first bridge you come to and walk into **Alfriston** where you will find several shops, pubs, restaurants and tearooms.

The Clergy House, next to Alfriston's church, was the first building purchased by the National Trust

Alfriston is one of the most popular villages in Sussex, with a long and narrow street lined with attractive old buildings, among the best of which are the 15th-century timber-framed George Inn and The Star Inn opposite. The parish church of St Andrew dates from the 14th century and is an imposing building, sometimes referred to as the 'Cathedral of the Downs' on account of its size. It stands on the village green, known as The Tye, and dwarfs the thatched Clergy House (National Trust) next door.

For the return leg of the walk make your way to the parish church, and take the footpath between the churchyard wall and the Clergy House. On coming to a crossing path turn right and follow the west bank of the river as it flows downstream to Exceat and Cuckmere Haven. At first this is a sluggish stream, but as you make progress and the valley becomes broader and more open below the steep slope of **High and Over**, so the river grows in confidence and becomes affected by the tides.

A few bridges span the river, but our route remains on the west (true right) bank; an easy walk with swans, ducks and geese for company. On occasion you may catch sight of a heron, or even a cormorant straying upstream. Rabbits honeycomb the banks; there may be cattle or sheep grazing the water meadows, and it's impossible to lose the way.

As you draw close to Exceat the path veers away from the river and brings you onto the A259. Turn left, and shortly after you come to **Exceat Bridge** by The Golden Galleon pub. Cross the bridge and wander ahead (pavement on the right-hand side of the road) to the Seven Sisters Country Park Visitor Centre to complete the circuit. ▶

Refreshments are available here.

WALK 7

Exceat Bridge to Cuckmere Haven and
Seaford Head

Distance	6½ miles (10.5km)
Map	OS Explorer 123 Eastbourne & Beachy Head 1:25,000
Start	Golden Galleon pub, Exceat Bridge (TV 514 994)
Access	By bus from Eastbourne, Seaford or Brighton: Exceat Bridge is on the A259 east of Seaford
Parking	Pay and display car parks near the Seven Sisters Country Park Visitor Centre, Exceat (TV 519 995)
Refreshments	Pub at Exceat Bridge

Some of the loveliest of all coastal views in the South of England can be enjoyed on this walk, which begins by following the Cuckmere River to its estuary between the guarding cliffs of the Seven Sisters and Seaford Head. It then strikes away from the coast, following a track to South Hill, then skirts a golf course to the edge of Seaford. The eastern end of the promenade now leads the way to the start of a glorious clifftop walk heading once more for Cuckmere Haven, from where an alternative path is taken back to Exceat Bridge.

Begin by walking through the car park of The Golden Galleon pub to a footpath flanked initially by hedges. When it forks veer left (the way ahead through a gate is used on the return) and very shortly come to the bank of the **Cuckmere River**. Heading south this raised path takes you above water meadows, which may be inundated at high tide, and leads directly to Cuckmere Haven, with its great shingle bank sliced by the escaping river. ◀ Turn right, go through a gate and up a track alongside one-time coastguards' cottages. Remain on the track as it veers to the right, rising gently onto **South Hill** with the broad, flat Cuckmere Valley seen off to the right. On reaching a car park by South Hill Barn (TV 504 981) veer left along a

To the left is a very fine view of the Seven Sisters seen in profile.

minor concrete road cutting between fields. This brings you to a golf course and a sign for Seaford Head Nature Reserve.

> Contained within the Seaford Head–Beachy Head SSSI, **Seaford Head Nature Reserve** extends to around 142 hectares. Over 250 plant species and more than 220 species of bird have been recorded here.

Turn hard right along the edge of the golf course and follow a grass path which soon slopes downhill between bushes. Before long it curves left away from the bushes to gain a view across Seaford and Seaford Bay towards Newhaven. At a junction of grass paths fork left across an open section. There are several crossing paths unmarked on the map, but each time you reach one simply continue ahead to regain the golf course.

Cross a fairway with care (beware golf balls), then go round the left-hand edge of a green to a second fairway. Cross this and pass between more greens to the continuing path which slopes downhill once more between bushes. A final fairway is crossed to gain a large meadow (an open green space) on the edge of Seaford. The path cuts across this to the far corner, although it's perfectly feasible to bear left on a short cut leading to Southdown Road. The 'official' route comes to a junction of roads at TV 491 986, where you then turn left along Southdown Road.

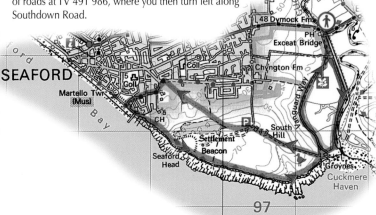

Bear right into Corsica Road, a residential street at the far end of which you keep ahead to reach the promenade. Turn left and after passing beach huts you will come to a sign indicating the route of the Vanguard Way. Walk up the path which leads onto **Seaford Head** (golf course to your left), with its beautiful views ahead to the Seven Sisters, and with the Belle Tout lighthouse clearly seen beyond Birling Gap.

Over the crown of Seaford Head the path descends into a 'dry valley' known as Cliff Bottom which effectively frames an exquisite view of the Seven Sisters. At the foot of the slope you come to Hope Gap where a stairway gives an opportunity to descend to the beach, should you wish. The continuing path now rises to join the track by the coastguards' cottages. Wander past these, go through the gate on the edge of Cuckmere Haven, then turn hard left, pass through a kissing gate and walk ahead on a grass path beside a fence. Beyond a second kissing gate the path is enclosed by fences.

Seaford Head grants an uninterrupted view of the Seven Sisters

58

When it forks, ignore the left-hand option and keep ahead between bushes.

Eventually pass through a gate and continue on a path which leads directly into the car park by The Golden Galleon.

The classic view of the Seven Sisters from the old coastguards' cottages above Cuckmere Haven

WALK 8

Alfriston to The Long Man of Wilmington

Distance	5 miles (8km)
Map	OS Explorer 123 Eastbourne & Beachy Head 1:25,000
Start	River Lane, Alfriston (TQ 521 032)
Access	By Cuckmere Community Bus, or Ramblerbus from Berwick Station (www.cuckmerebus.freeuk.com or ☎ 01323 870920). Nearest railway stations at Berwick and Seaford
Parking	Public car parks at northern end of Alfriston village (TQ 521 033)
Refreshments	Pubs, cafés, restaurants and shops in Alfriston, pub in Wilmington

This gentle circular walk climbs onto the slopes of Windover Hill, and passes below the Long Man of Wilmington before descending to the Cuckmere Valley and returning to Alfriston by way of the earthworks of Burlough Castle, and a short stroll alongside the river.

From the Market Cross at the northern end of Alfriston High Street, walk down River Lane (sign for the South Downs Way), and at the bottom turn right along the bank of the River

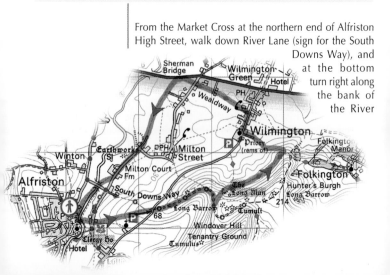

Cuckmere. On coming to a footbridge, cross to the east bank and, ignoring footpaths to right and left, keep ahead as far as a narrow lane opposite the attractive Great Meadow Barn (Plonk Barn on the 1:25,000 OS map). Turn right and, after a few paces, take a footpath on the left, signed to Jevington.

Halfway up the slope, bear left through a line of trees, then angle up and across the sloping field to a gap in a hedge. Through this gap continue across the next field. Off to the right the spire of Lullington Church, partly hidden among trees, can be seen nearby. On the far side of the field a stile leads onto a crossing path where you turn right. This is on the route of the South Downs Way. Very shortly arrive at another narrow lane beside a small parking area at TQ 532 032.

Cross directly ahead onto a continuing chalk path rising up the flank of Windover Hill. Pass a flat-topped underground reservoir, go through a gate and immediately turn left onto the crest of the Downs to gain a view across the Cuckmere Valley to the long line of the South Downs stretching north-westward, forming an effective wall to the low-lying spread of the Weald.

Follow a fence-line for a few paces, then take a footpath off to the right. Keep ahead at a crossing path, then go through a bridle gate and wander along the steep west slope. When the path forks, keep on the upper branch to pass below the **Long Man of Wilmington**.

THE LONG MAN OF WILMINGTON

The Long Man of Wilmington is said to be England's largest chalk figure. Cut into the Downland slope facing north, he is 226ft (69m) long and with outstretched arms holds a 250ft (76m) staff in each hand. Although his origin is unknown, he was traditionally thought to have been created in the Bronze Age, some 4000 years ago. Others speculate that he was carved by the Saxons, but whoever was responsible for this most famous of Sussex figures, he was cleverly designed in such a way that he is never seriously foreshortened from wherever he is studied, despite the steepness of the hill.

Ignore the path which descends to a gate and continue ahead on what is part of the Wealdway long distance path. This eventually brings you to another gate by some trees. Through this turn left on a broad sunken path which leads to **Wilmington** High Street opposite the 12th-century church of St Mary and St Peter. Beside the church stands an ancient yew tree thought to be about 1600 years old. Turn right and walk through the village to a telephone box, where you then turn left along a tarmac drive. ◀ When the road curves a little to the right, leave the drive for a footpath going ahead, then over a stile follow the right-hand edge of a field to a gap in the hedge. Go through this, then with the hedge to your left maintain direction, and at the far side of the field go through a small plantation and into another open meadow. Across this pass alongside an attractive flint-walled converted barn, and continue across interlinking fields following **Wealdway** signs to reach a country road at TQ 538 049.

Cross a stile into another field directly ahead, and follow the right-hand hedgerow to an oak tree. Cross another stile and turn left for a few paces, not far from the

For refreshments continue along the High Street a short distance to the village pub.

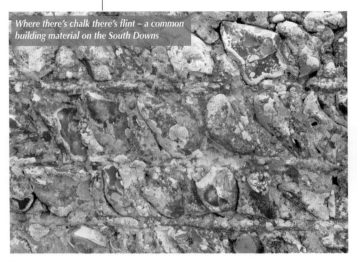

Where there's chalk there's flint – a common building material on the South Downs

busy A27. Bear left across a small field to yet another stile giving access to a sloping field, where you keep along its left-hand boundary with Berwick church seen at the foot of the Downs off to your right.

Pass alongside some ruined flint walls, and by way of linking fields come to the **earthworks** of Burlough Castle, after which the way goes along a hedge-lined track. This eventually spills onto a lane at a bend on the outskirts of Milton Street. Walk ahead along the lane, but at the far end of the boundary wall of **Milton Court Farm**, go through a kissing gate on the right, and over two linking fields to another narrow lane. Turn right, cross a bridge over the Cuckmere, then follow a raised footpath on the left to accompany the river back to Alfriston, and come to River Lane where the walk began.

In the distance, The Long man of Wilmington, icon of the Downs

WALK 9

Alfriston to Bostal Hill, Alciston and Berwick

Distance	7 miles (11km)
Map	OS Explorer 123 Eastbourne & Beachy Head 1:25,000
Start	Star Lane, Alfriston (TQ 521 031)
Access	By Cuckmere Community Bus, or Ramblerbus from Berwick Station (www.cuckmerebus.freeuk.com or ☎ 01323 870920). Nearest railway stations at Berwick and Seaford
Parking	Public car parks at northern end of Alfriston village (TQ 521 033)
Refreshments	Pubs, cafés, restaurants and shops in Alfriston, pubs in Alciston and Berwick

Extensive views over the Weald, and two interesting villages, are among the highlights of this circular walk which follows sections of the South Downs Way and the Vanguard Way, and adopts a length of farm track running along the foot of the Downs.

Arlington Reservoir can be seen in the vast expanse of the Weald stretched out below.

In the centre of Alfriston by the historic Star Inn leave the High Street and walk along Star Lane on the route of the South Downs Way. At crossroads continue ahead up Kings Ride, and when this ends follow a chalk and flint track rising between bushes. Near the head of the slope the track reveals a fine view over the Weald. Shortly after, take a narrow bridleway which cuts ahead while the track veers left. A few paces later cross another track, go through a bridle gate and walk ahead alongside a fence reaching across the Downs. ◄

As the walk progresses, the view to the left grows in extent to include Cuckmere Haven, Seaford Head and Newhaven, although the Weald to the right is lost for a while. Remaining on the South Downs Way the path eventually brings you onto **Bostal Hill**, a very fine vantage point,

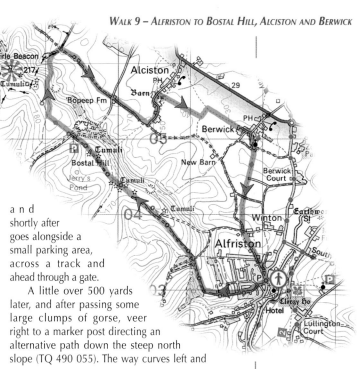

a n d shortly after goes alongside a small parking area, across a track and ahead through a gate.

A little over 500 yards later, and after passing some large clumps of gorse, veer right to a marker post directing an alternative path down the steep north slope (TQ 490 055). The way curves left and

The patchwork Weald lies below Bostal Hill (Walk 10)

65

descends at an easy gradient, with exquisite views overlooking the Weald, with Charleston Farmhouse to the north, Upper Barn below, and Alciston and Berwick huddled among fields or trees to the east.

At the foot of the slope the path traces the edge of a small woodland and out to a crossing track where you turn right. This track, or farm road, leads almost all the way to Alfriston, although we do not follow it throughout. Soon pass the large flintstone Upper Barn, and shortly after, a small cottage unmarked on the O.S. map. The way continues between large fields at the foot of the Downs and reaches **Bopeep Farm** beside the narrow lane that climbs to the car park near Bostal Hill.

Snug at the foot of the Downs, **Bopeep Farmhouse** offers B&B in an idyllic location (☎ 01323 871299).

The Norman church in Alciston

A little under ½ mile (800m) ahead you come to a junction of tracks marked by an attractive three-sided Millennium seat. Turn left to visit Alciston. The narrow

lane curves round a medieval tithe barn with a massive roof, and soon after comes to a crossing path with the Parish church seen to the right.

Alciston is a tiny village with a medieval tithe barn, a plain Norman church, and a dovecote nearby that is said to have been built by the monks of Battle Abbey, possibly in the 14th century. The village has some very attractive thatched cottages and the popular Rose Cottage Inn a short distance north of the church.

Take the fence-enclosed footpath towards the church, then over a squeeze stile on the left follow a path round the churchyard wall. Cross another stile and turn right, pass through a gap and turn left alongside a hedge, now walking towards Berwick church whose spire can be seen among trees ahead. On reaching a second large field, turn left along its headland, then right at the corner to resume the approach to Berwick on a grass path. This brings you to woodland where you continue ahead past the buildings of Church Farm to reach a T-junction of lanes (TQ 518 052). Bear right and walk towards the Parish church of **Berwick**, dedicated to St Michael and All Angels (if you need refreshment, turn left at the junction to find The Cricketers Arms).

The 12th-century **Berwick church** contains a series of murals created during the Second World War by Duncan Grant, Vanessa Bell and her son Quentin Bell, members of the Bloomsbury Set who lived at Charleston Farmhouse (see Walk 11). The wall paintings depict biblical scenes set against a Sussex landscape (see **www.berwickchurch.org.uk**). North of the church the village pub, The Cricketers Arms, is a flint cottage with a pleasant garden.

Just inside the churchyard go out by way of a kissing gate on the left, turn right in a small field, then right again between hedges and through another kissing gate, now on the Vanguard Way. Bear right for a few paces on a grass crossing track, then left on a footpath through an open field. At the far side go through a gate in a hedge, and continue ahead through linking fields to join the track/farm road previously followed as far as the outskirts of Alciston.

After a very short distance come to a narrow tarmac lane flanked by hedges. Keep ahead and this will bring you into Alfriston near the Market Cross at the northern end of the High Street.

Alfriston is known to have been settled since prehistoric times, and being sited in the Cuckmere Valley at a junction of tracks coming from Newhaven, Lewes and Jevington made it a natural centre as a market. The village was also once a haunt of smugglers, but today it's noted for the number of fine old buildings that line the High Street, among them the 15th-century George Inn, and The Star opposite – both timber-framed, as is the thatched Clergy House next to the parish church on The Tye.

A short diversion from the Bopeep car park leads to a memorable vantage point (Walk 10)

WALK 10

Bopeep to Bishopstone

Distance	7½ miles (12km)
Map	OS Explorer 123 Eastbourne & Beachy Head 1:25,000
Start	Bopeep Car Park near Bostal Hill (TQ 494 051)
Access	Via Bopeep Lane off A27, ½ mile northwest of Alciston. Nearest railway station at Berwick
Parking	At start of walk
Refreshments	None on route

The vast open spaces and huge panoramic views for which the eastern Downs are so justifiably feted are a major feature of this walk, but a slight diversion to visit the magnificent Saxon church at Bishopstone is highly recommended, for it's one of the gems of the region that will surely leave a lasting memory for all but the most hardened of cynics.

Bopeep car park, where this walk begins, is situated on the lip of the Downs a little northwest of Bostal Hill, and is reached by a narrow, mostly single-track lane off the busy A27. A few paces from the car park one of the finest views in the South Downs National Park may be had overlooking the patchwork landscape of the Weald.

Leave the car park at the end farthest away from the entrance, and follow the track of the South Downs Way, heading southeast, rising to **Bostal Hill** whose high point is marked by a low burial mound, from which a tremendous view may be had looking across the Weald. Beyond Bostal Hill the way slopes gently downhill, then forks. Branch right on a grassy bridleway. On coming to a bridle gate, pass through and continue ahead, and as you wander downhill Seaford may be seen ahead to the left, and Newhaven ahead to the right, while the open spaces of the Downs spread out on either side.

At the foot of the slope the way narrows to a clear chalk trail that begins to climb between bushes. On reaching the

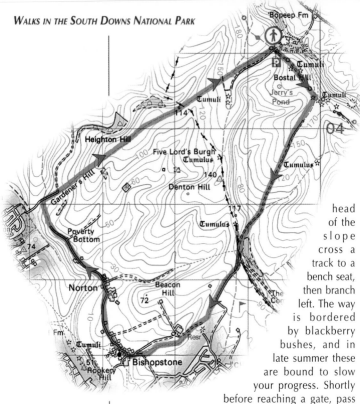

head of the slope cross a track to a bench seat, then branch left. The way is bordered by blackberry bushes, and in late summer these are bound to slow your progress. Shortly before reaching a gate, pass through a gap in the right-hand hedge, then walk along the left-hand edge of a large field. To the southwest the spire of Bishopstone church may be seen rising above the trees in a hollow.

On coming to the end of the field squeeze through a gap into a second field, and maintain direction. At the corner of this field bear right and continue along its left-hand edge to the next corner where you'll find a kissing gate overlooking large barns. Through the gate keep to the upper edge of a sloping meadow where the way is led between bushes once more. Shortly after crossing a stile come onto a track which slopes downhill to pass between converted farm buildings in the small village of

Dating from about AD950, St Andrew's church at Bishopstone is one of the gems of the South Downs

Bishopstone, where you arrive at a road just east of the church at TQ 474 009. Turn right for the continuing walk, but a diversion to visit the lovely old Saxon church of St Andrew's is highly recommended.

ST ANDREW'S CHURCH

Open on Wednesdays, Saturdays and Sundays (for services), St Andrew's Church is one of the real gems of the South Downs. It is thought that the Nave was built before AD950, and the porch, once used as a side chapel, is also of Saxon origin – note the Saxon sundial above the door, inscribed with the name 'Eadric'. The Chancel and Sanctuary are Norman, built in the 12th century, and the whole place is kept in immaculate condition. Ten centuries of use have given it a continuing aura of peace, calm and grace. Its setting is perfect, and a visit will add perspective to your wanderings.

Follow the quiet road out of Bishopstone for about ½ mile (800m) to the few houses of Norton. Branch left when the road forks and soon come to a sign announcing this as a private no through road. There is, however, a public right of way (a bridleway) along it, so continue ahead along an area known as Norton Bottom, with a steep slope on the left and the Downs spreading to the right.

After passing some works buildings the tarmac road becomes a track, and when this forks keep ahead, ignoring that which curves to the right. The track becomes a narrow bridleway rising gently between bushes and trees in **Poverty Bottom**. At the head of the slope come to a crossing bridleway (TQ 461 030) and a panoramic view which includes Seaford Head to the southeast.

Turn right and follow the bridleway downhill where it forks in the open grassy area of Stump Bottom. Ignore the left branch which goes to Blackcap Hill, and keep ahead, now rising up the right-hand edge of a field on **Gardener's Hill**. Through a gate continue uphill on a downland meadow spreading over **Heighton Hill**. On the far side of this go through a second gate in a fence and maintain direction ahead. In the far right-hand corner a bridle gate leads the way into a high meadow which slopes downhill to right and left. After passing through yet another bridle gate a marker post will be seen a short way ahead and slightly to the right at TQ 488 047.

This post marks an indistinct four-way crossing of bridleways. Ignore that which crosses from right to left and wander slightly right ahead (aiming northeast) through a large open downland meadow. There is little indication of the route on the ground, and the far boundary is not always visible, but you should make for the top right-hand corner, joining a track shortly before coming to a final gate a few paces from the Bopeep car park.

WALK 11

Glynde to Beddingham Hill, Firle Beacon and Bostal Hill

Distance	11 miles (17.5km)
Map	OS Explorer 123 Eastbourne & Beachy Head 1:25,000
Start	Glynde Railway Station (TQ 457 086)
Access	By rail: on the Lewes to Eastbourne line. By road: Glynde is located northeast of the A26/A27 junction on a minor road to Ringmer, and is served by bus from Lewes and Alfriston
Parking	Public car park at entrance to Glynde recreation ground, north of the station (TQ 457 088)
Refreshments	Pub, shop and tearoom in Glynde; pubs in Alciston and Firle

The longest route in the book, this is a walk of two halves: a section of the South Downs Way being followed eastward along the crest of the Downs, then a westbound lowland walk which passes through two villages, goes alongside one-time home of 'The Bloomsbury Group' of writers and artists, and wanders through the parkland of majestic Firle Place. Given reasonable conditions, views can be enthralling for most of the way, with a contrast of rolling, expansive downland, and the immense sweep of the chequerboard Weald. Refreshments are available at strategic points along the way.

From Glynde Station pass The Trevor Arms pub and wander south alongside a minor road to reach the A27, which you cross (with care) to a narrow lane directly ahead. Still heading south towards the Downs, with the tall radio masts on Beddingham Hill in view, pass a few houses, after which the lane becomes partly surfaced as it rises between hedges. After going through a gate the slope steepens, with views opening to either side as the lane/track angles along the eastern edge of gorse-lined Ellman's Combe. The banks are covered in cow-slips in springtime. Above this you come onto the crest

73

of the Downs by crosstracks and a SDW finger post at TQ 455 059.

Turn left and follow the SDW eastwards, skirting along the left-hand side of the radio masts, and beyond these over close-cropped grass as the broad-backed Downs roll away into the distance. Easy walking leads to a car park and another

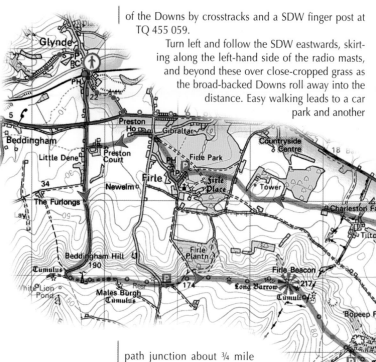

path junction about ¾ mile from the radio masts. Walk through the car park and out by a bridle gate to continue along the SDW with a view onto Firle (which will be visited later in the walk) at the foot of the Downs. Passing several burial mounds the way comes to **Firle Beacon** whose trig point stands just to the left of the trail (TQ 485 059). At 713ft (217m) this is the highest point on the South Downs east of the Ouse Valley.

On coming to a second car park (Bopeep) keep ahead along a flint track leading to Bostal Hill. ◀ Over this, and about ½ mile (800m) beyond the car park note a finger post indicating a crossing path. Leave the SDW here and turn left. The path may not be immediately

Paragliders are sometimes launched from here.

evident on the ground, but in a few paces as you crest the Downs, you will see a stile in a fence just below. Cross this and take a path sloping downhill to the left. ▶ At the foot of the slope cross another stile, go down steps and along a sunken path between trees. This eventually eases into the left-hand field, then onto a farm road where you turn right. Shortly after, come to a junction of farm roads/tracks and turn left to enter **Alciston**.

A huge panoramic view reveals the Weald spreading far to the north, east and west. Arlington Reservoir lies to the northeast; the village of Alciston lies below.

Nestling at the foot of the Downs, **Alciston** is an old village, first mentioned in the Domesday Book. It has a number of attractive buildings, including a medieval tithe barn and dovecote, a Norman church whose graveyard is a riot of wild flowers in springtime, and several picturesque thatched cottages.

Walk through the village, passing The Rose Cottage Inn, and when the lane starts to curve break away left on a footpath by some trees, go through a kissing gate and enter a meadow with a splendid view of the South Downs. On the far side go through a second kissing gate and over a minor stream into another meadow. Walk ahead alongside the left-hand hedge, then curve right on reaching the far boundary, to find a five-bar gate and yet another kissing gate in the bottom corner. Through this go up a slope with a hedgerow on your right and come onto a narrow lane at TQ 506 065.

Turn left for a few paces, then join a concrete drive on the right. This curves left and eventually leads to a house named Keepers, which stands on the edge of Tilton Wood. Maintain direction beyond the end of the drive and wander through a series of meadows linked by gates until you reach a narrow lane opposite the drive to Charleston Farm. Keep ahead along the drive, pass **Charleston Farmhouse** and continue on a farm track which leads beyond it.

Charleston Farmhouse is an attractive 17th-century building which, in 1916, became the home of artists Vanessa Bell and Duncan Grant, who used it as a gathering place for the Bloomsbury Group of writers, artists and intellectuals – most notably Leonard and Virginia Woolf (Vanessa Bell's sister), Lytton Strachey and John Maynard Keynes. The house was decorated throughout by Bell and Grant in Post-Impressionist style, and is now open to the public: April to end of October, afternoons from Wednesday to Saturday plus Sundays and Bank Holiday Mondays (☎ 01323 811265 **www.charleston.org.uk**).

Wandering along the track Firle Tower may be seen on the crown of a hill ahead. Go through a gate and keep ahead along the left-hand side of a meadow, with Compton Wood off to the right. Shortly before reaching the far side of the meadow, pass through a gap on the left, then through a gate turn right. Over a minor stream veer half-left to another gate in a hedgerow. Now rise gently across a field and through a gap into an adjacent field where you pass below the circular, three-storey folly of **Firle Tower** (TQ 482 073). On the far side cross a private drive leading to the tower.

On the approach to Firle, an open view shows Mount Caburn ahead

Through a woodland shaw emerge to a glorious view which shows a vast sweep of field, meadow and parkland, the abrupt flank of the Downs spreading west, Mount Caburn backing the valley of Glynde Reach, and a first glimpse of Firle Place ahead. Bear right round the bottom edge of a wood, then veer left across a field corner, and pass between two tile-hung and flint-walled houses. Cross a narrow lane and go through a gate into **Firle Park**, where marker posts direct the way. On the north side of Firle Place a finger post directs the way to Firle church, and across the parkland you come to a track which leads into Firle village.

Firle Place is a large, handsome Georgian mansion with the original Tudor house, thought to have been built in the 15th century by Sir John Gage, encased within it. Set in magnificent parkland, the house has been in the Gage family throughout its history. It is open to the public on Sunday, Wednesday and Thursday afternoons, from June to September, and at Easter and Spring Bank Holiday on Sunday and Monday (☎ 01273 858307 **www.firleplace.co.uk**). The nearby village of Firle is served by bus from Lewes and Alfriston.

Passing several houses come into the heart of the village beside Firle Stores (the OS 1:25,000 map calls it West Firle, but it's generally known simply as Firle). The church, which is part-Norman, part 13th and 15th century in construction, is off to the left, but we bear right and walk along the street as far as The Ram Inn, then go down a track along its right-hand side. Entering a meadow area, with the cricket pitch to your right, branch left to a kissing gate immediately beside a tennis court. Now cross a meadow to its far corner, where another gate can be seen on the edge of woods. Out of this gate cross to a lodge gate and a junction of country roads. Directly ahead there's a gravel drive at TQ 466 078.

The drive becomes a track between fields, and on reaching a Dutch barn it curves left then right where you

Impressive Firle Place is seen from the walk across parkland to Firle village

follow a slightly raised footpath through a large open field, with Mount Caburn to the right, and Beddingham Hill on the left. A gate in a hedgerow leads into a narrow meadow, across which you pass through another gate and across a larger meadow come onto a drive at **Preston Court Farm**. This leads to a familiar lane where you turn right, and shortly after cross the A27 (take care) and follow the outward route back to Glynde.

WALK 12

Glynde to Mount Caburn and Saxon Cross

Distance	6 miles (9.5km)
Maps	OS Explorer 122 Brighton & Hove and 123 Eastbourne & Beachy Head 1:25,000
Start	Glynde Railway Station (TQ 457 086)
Access	By rail: on the Lewes to Eastbourne line. By road: Glynde is located northeast of the A26/A27 junction on a minor road to Ringmer, and is served by a bus route from Lewes and Alfriston
Parking	Public car park at entrance to Glynde recreation ground, north of the station (TQ 457 088)
Refreshments	Pub, shop and tearoom in Glynde

East of Lewes an isolated section of steep-walled Downs, conveniently ringed by roads, gives some rewarding walks, with surprisingly secluded countryside and far-reaching views. On the southern edge of this downland block, the Iron Age hillfort site of Mount Caburn is a notable vantage point and an exciting launch pad for paragliding enthusiasts. The western edge gives birdseye views onto Lewes rooftops; the northern slopes plunge towards Ringmer, while from the eastern side the world-famous opera venue of Glyndebourne can be seen among the trees. But in the 'heartland' of these Downs, a narrow dry valley is squeezed by abrupt sheep-grazed slopes devoid of habitation yet inspiring to wander through.

Out of the railway station cross Glynde Reach, the eastern arm of the River Ouse, and passing the recreation ground on your left walk into Glynde village. Turn left into Ranscombe Lane and, a few paces beyond Glynde Stores, cross a stile on the right and follow a footpath rising through three interlinking meadows, from which you can see, across the valley to the south, Beddingham Hill with its tall radio masts. At the head of the second meadow a bench seat provides an excuse for a rest with

The third large meadow is rich in wild flowers in spring and early summer.

Glynde seen directly below and the Weald spreading far to the north. ◀ On reaching the head of the slope you come to another stile in a long fence (TQ 445 093). Before crossing the stile turn left in order to visit **Mount Caburn**, which has a bench seat on the south side overlooking the River Ouse, then return to the stile for the continuing walk.

> **Mount Caburn**, or The Caburn as it appears on some maps, clearly shows two defensive dykes and the earthen ramparts of an Iron Age hillfort created in the third century BC by a Celtic tribe that occupied this corner of the Downs. It is thought that some 70 families lived on this elevated site, which stands 492ft (150m) above sea level, and archaeological discoveries made at the site are kept in Lewes Museum. Mount Caburn is protected as a National Nature Reserve.

The dry valley of Oxteddle Bottom lies below Mount Caburn

Cross the stile and go down the slope towards a narrow cleave, or dry valley, known as Oxteddle Bottom. At

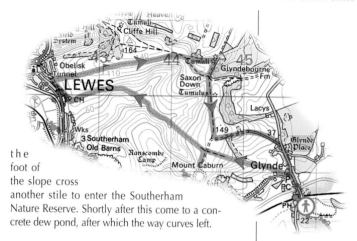

the
foot of
the slope cross
another stile to enter the Southerham
Nature Reserve. Shortly after this come to a concrete dew pond, after which the way curves left.

The **Southerham Nature Reserve** in Oxteddle Bottom
was once part of a working farm that now supports a
rich variety of butterflies and chalk grassland flowers,
including several species of orchid. For more information contact Sussex Wildlife Trust on ☎ 01273 492630
or go to **www.sussexwt.org.uk**.

A marker post now directs the footpath up the right-
hand slope, but over a stile the way veers left, and in a
few paces it forks. The lower option goes to Southerham
Farm, but we take the right branch up the slope ahead
and, rising across the downland flank, negotiate more
stiles on the way to a field corner near the **clubhouse** of
Lewes Golf Club at TQ 426 099.

From the small clubhouse car park, go down the
slope on a narrow footpath beside the drive, from which
you soon gain views of Lewes, and directly onto the
rooftops of houses beside the River Ouse. The gradient steepens and, immediately before reaching the first
house, you turn right onto a track, and a few paces later
ascend a flight of steps among trees. All the height lost
below the clubhouse now has to be regained, and you
eventually emerge from the trees on the edge of the golf

course a short distance to the right of an **obelisk**. One path cuts left along the golf course boundary, but our route crosses directly ahead over a series of greens and fairways, guided by marker posts. Note the signs that give warning as to which direction golfers may be driving. ◄

Beware of flying golf balls.

LEWES

Lewes commands the Ouse Valley. This, the county town of East Sussex, boasts one of the earliest of Norman castles, built by William de Warenne after he was given the Rape of Lewes by William the Conqueror. Although the stronghold was built to protect the town against invaders sailing up the Ouse estuary, the castle was never really put to the test. In May 1264 the Battle of Lewes was fought on the Downs west of the town, between Henry III's men and those of Simon de Montfort. Such was the carnage that when navvies were constructing the railway in 1846, they came upon the mass grave of those who were slaughtered nearly 600 years earlier; the bones filled 13 waggons. Lewes is basically medieval in layout, but it was heavily altered in Georgian times. Daniel Defoe described it as 'a fine pleasant town, well built, agreeably situated in the middle of an open champagne country.' A century later, in 1822, William Cobbett found it to be 'a model of solidity and neatness … the people well-dressed; and, though last not least, the girls remarkably pretty.'

The way across the golf course eventually brings you to a stile giving onto downland once more directly below the unseen crown of **Cliffe Hill**, which is screened by gorse bushes. Walk directly ahead through two adjoining meadows linked by a gate. From the path you can see down into both Bible Bottom and Oxteddle Bottom, whose concrete dew pond is clearly visible. At the far side of the second meadow go through another gate to find the low marker stone known as Saxon Cross a few paces beyond it. ◄

From this downland crest you gain a fine view north over the Weald, with Ringmer lying below.

You are now faced with two options. One faint grass path heads to the right across Saxon Down; the other recommended route maintains direction after coming through the gate, and goes down the right-hand side of a wooded slope to another concrete dew pond at TQ 446 106. Just beyond it there is a field gate beside a wood.

Do not pass through this gate, but turn hard right round the dew pond and follow a chalk track which rises gently alongside a fence and soon passes what appears to be a small one-time chalk quarry. Beyond the quarry the track forks. Branch left and soon the track is joined by a path from the right – this is the alternative route from Saxon Cross.

Just ahead cross a stile beside a field gate and maintain direction. The track having ended at the gate, you now walk along a grass path rising across the Downs heading south to a second stile and gate. Beyond this come onto a downland crown to gain a direct view of Mount Caburn ahead. On coming to a marker post to the left of a field gate, turn left and shortly after come onto a track sloping downhill among banks of cowslips and celandines in springtime, with bluebells in the right-hand woodland. When the woodland ends, a bench seat exploits a fine view to south and east, while the track continues until it reaches the northern end of **Glynde** near Home Farm (TQ 455 094). Turn right and walk into the village, passing Glynde Place and the parish church on the left.

GLYNDE

Glynde takes its name from gline, meaning 'a fenced enclosure' – possibly a reference to the fortified site of Mount Caburn. The village has some pleasant cottages and an attractive forge, and standing next to Glynde Place, the church of St Mary the Virgin was built between 1763 and 1765, on the site of an earlier medieval place of worship, by Bishop Richard Trevor, who lived next door. A short distance up the road towards Ringmer, Glyndebourne was opened as an opera house in 1934 by John and Audrey Christie, and has now gained an international reputation, as much for its setting as for the quality of the productions staged there.

WALK 13

Southease Station to Rodmell and Telscombe

Distance	7½ miles (12km)
Map	OS Explorer 122 Brighton & Hove 1:25,000
Start	Southease Station (TQ 431 055)
Access	By train on the Lewes to Newhaven line. Buses from both towns also serve Rodmell (not Sundays)
Parking	With discretion on minor road east of Southease
Refreshments	None

The walk begins and ends along a footpath embankment beside the River Ouse – once a major waterway, as the 1:25,000 map clearly illustrates – whose valley is now a low-lying area of reed-lined channels rich in birdlife. The walk then visits Rodmell, the flint-walled village in which novelist Virginia Woolf and her husband Leonard once lived, before climbing onto the Downs at Mill Hill, which has a wide-open vista and endless horizons. Heading roughly southward the walk now makes for the tiny village of Telscombe, before turning east to cross Bullock Down, then swooping downhill among blackthorn bushes and slopes of violet and cowslip in springtime, to regain the west bank of the Ouse once more.

This low valley of the Ouse carves a trench through the South Downs between Itford Hill (on the east) and Mill Hill to the west.

Leaving Southease railway halt, wander along the narrow lane heading west towards the village, whose church is barely glimpsed among trees, and a few paces after crossing a bridge spanning the **River Ouse**, turn right onto a raised footpath and follow the river upstream. ◀ Swans, Little egrets, cormorants and waders may be seen on the main river, but elsewhere the reed-lined drainage channels are often the scene of a feeding frenzy as smaller birds dart to and fro after seeds and insects.

Until the Middle Ages, the **River Ouse** entered the English Channel at Seaford, which was then the port for

84

Lewes. But a great storm in 1579 changed the course of the river which found a 'new haven' a little to the west – the Newhaven of today.

About a mile (1.5km) after joining the river bank go through a kissing gate, then descend from the embankment and follow a track heading away from the river alongside a reed-fringed channel. Without diverting from it, the track leads into Rodmell. Walk directly ahead through the village, passing a number of attractive flint-walled cottages, and a rather plain, white weatherboard cottage known as **Monk's House** on the left.

The brick- and flint-built **Monk's House** was the country home of Leonard and Virginia Woolf from 1919. Its rooms display examples of the work of fellow Bloomsbury Group artists, Duncan Grant and Vanessa Bell, and it was from here that Virginia, suffering mental illness in 1941, walked down to the River Ouse and took her own life. The house is now owned by the National Trust, and is open to the public on Wednesday and Saturday afternoons from April until the end of October (For information ☎ 01372 453401 – NT Regional Office).

At the southern end of the village come to a T-junction, cross slightly left ahead and walk along Mill

The flint-walled church in Telscombe

Lane, rising gently between houses. As you progress, so the lane narrows between hedges before ending at the entrance to a large house on **Mill Hill** (TQ 413 054). Through a gate you come to a signpost announcing the South Downs Way. Suddenly a wide vista reveals a great sweep of downland; immediately ahead the hillside plunges steeply into Cricketing Bottom.

Turn left along the route of the SDW, following a vague path directed by a marker post. The way slopes downhill and goes through a gate with untidy farm buildings seen ahead. Bear left to reach a farm track where a signpost directs the SDW to the left. Leave that route, turn right and wander along the track to pass between farm buildings. Remain on the continuing track for about ½ mile (800m), and shortly after it forks, with one breaking to the right, go through a gate on the left and walk down a slope of meadowland alongside a fence, then bear right round the boundary, now on a narrow track which brings you to a metalled lane. Walk ahead along the lane, and shortly enter the small village of **Telscombe**. Immediately before coming to the church turn left along yet another track.

Just past **Telscombe** church a row of cottages has been converted to a simple, self-catering youth hostel (TQ 405 033).

When the track forks after a few paces, take the upper option. This is tree-lined, with lovely open downland spreading to north and south. Eventually pass alongside several houses and keep ahead. After the last house walk along a narrow footpath enclosed by hedges, then through a gate to another big open view with the tall radio masts on Beddingham Hill seen to the northeast across the Ouse Valley.

Wander slightly right ahead across a meadow corner to a gate. Through this a fence-lined path twists downhill among scrub, then you pass through another gate and cross a final strip of meadow onto a track where you turn left. Easy walking brings you to a road by the beautifully

Leaving Telscombe the walk takes a tree-lined track onto more downland

converted flint-walled Chapel Barn about ½ mile (800m) from **Piddinghoe**. Cross the road with care, and over a stile come onto the west bank of the River Ouse once more. Bear left and keep on the embankment footpath for a little over a mile (1.5km), until arriving at the road bridge spanning the river between Southease and the railway halt where the walk began. Turn right for the station.

WALK 14

Cooksbridge to Plumpton Plain and Buckland Bank

Distance	10 miles (16km)
Map	OS Explorer 122 Brighton & Hove 1:25,000
Start	Cooksbridge Railway Station (TQ 401 135)
Access	By train: Cooksbridge is on the London to Lewes line. By road: the village stands astride the A275 about 2½ miles north of Lewes, and is served by bus from that town
Parking	Limited parking by the station
Refreshments	Café in Cooksbridge

The walk begins with a leisurely approach across low-lying farmland to the foot of the Downs, followed by a steady ascent to the crest just east of Blackcap. The way then makes a counter-clockwise tour, with long views a permanent feature. Plumpton Plain is a mixture of arable and downland, but the vast majority of the walk is over the cropped grass of Stanmer and Balmer Downs.

Out of Cooksbridge Station head south alongside the A275 for about 150 yards, then turn right into Beechwood Lane. Very shortly enter the recreation ground and turn right: pass through the children's play area, cross a stile in the hedge and continue through a field walking parallel with Beechwood Lane until you reach the far side. Turn left along the boundary, with a large pond now on your right.

At the end of the field cross a ditch and walk across the next field to a stile seen about 30 yards to the right of a gate. You now enter a large open meadow and walk across it towards **Tulleys Wells Farm**, where you come to another stile in a fence. Over a narrow track a second stile gives access to another meadow which you cross to yet another stile leading onto the farm drive. Walk down the drive to an attractive timber-framed house by the B2116 at TQ 392 130. Turn right.

Follow the road through a wooded area for about ½ mile (800m), but as it begins to curve to the right, cross to a drive at **Courthouse Farm**.

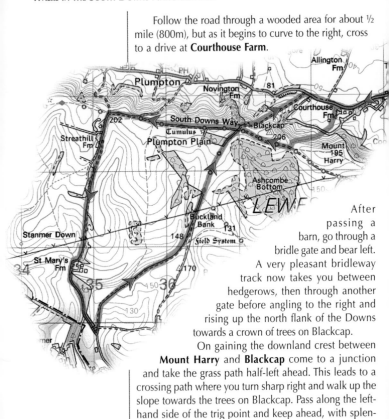

After passing a barn, go through a bridle gate and bear left. A very pleasant bridleway track now takes you between hedgerows, then through another gate before angling to the right and rising up the north flank of the Downs towards a crown of trees on Blackcap.

On gaining the downland crest between **Mount Harry** and **Blackcap** come to a junction and take the grass path half-left ahead. This leads to a crossing path where you turn sharp right and walk up the slope towards the trees on Blackcap. Pass along the left-hand side of the trig point and keep ahead, with splendid views all around. In springtime tiny cowslips show their delicate yellow heads in the cropped grass, while large gorse bushes blaze golden. Between the bushes you gain big views over the Weald. West of Blackcap come to a field gate with a bridle gate next to it, and exchange National Trust land for the track of the South Downs Way.

The fence-lined track heads west across **Plumpton Plain**: arable fields to the left, grassland on the right. After almost a mile another track cuts back to the right and descends to Plumpton, which has a large agricultural college and the Lutyens-designed Plumpton Place, but is probably better known for its racecourse, which is found north of the village. We, however, ignore this track and continue ahead along the SDW for another 350 yards until, just before coming to a very narrow crossing road which leads to Streathill Farm, we go through a bridle gate on the left, and walk down the right-hand edge of a large sweeping meadow that falls away into Faulkner's Bottom.

South of the track across **Plumpton Plain** two major sites that were part of a Bronze Age settlement are clearly shown on the OS 1:25,000 map. Each contains banked enclosures that were linked by tracks, while along the downland crest between Offham Hill near Lewes, and the Clayton Windmills, a series of burial mounds give further clues to the ancient history of the South Downs.

Descending below Blackcap another big view opens across the Weald

The chalk track below Blackcap

Immediately below **Streathill Farm** (TQ 351 125) go through another bridle gate and follow a track sloping downhill alongside a fence. Passing Horseshoe Plantation continue down through a field gate to reach a group of buildings leading to **St Mary's Farm** in Shambledean Bottom. The track now becomes a farm drive rising alongside another woodland, soon gaining sight of a group of University of Sussex buildings at Falmer. Eventually the farm drive slopes downhill, but very shortly you turn left into a lay-by from where a bridleway heads north, with part of the ruined Ridge Farm seen on the left.

Within a few paces ignore a track heading to the right towards Balmer Farm and keep ahead, rising between large arable fields. On Waterpit Hill the way forks, with one path going through a gate on the left. Ignore this and remain on the fenced bridleway, with panoramic views stretching far off in all directions. Eventually join a chalk track and continue ahead along Buckland Bank, and a few paces after passing beneath high voltage cables, rejoin the South Downs Way. When this brings you to crossing tracks, where the SDW turns hard left along

Plumpton Plain, go through a gate on the right onto the National Trust land of Blackcap, which should be familiar from the early part of the walk. Immediately turn left on a faint grass path.

Cowslips adorn the downland slopes in springtime

This soon becomes a sunken chalk track descending between high banks extravagent with cowslips, and with lovely views across the Weald once more. Pass below Blackcap's crown and eventually come onto the B2116 at TQ 378 130. Cross the road to where the grass verge enables you to walk in comfort and safety. Turn right to wander past **Courthouse Farm**, and through woodland until arriving at the drive leading to **Tulleys Wells Farm**, where you retrace the first part of the walk back to Cooksbridge Station.

WALK 15

*Hassocks to the Clayton Windmills
and Ditchling Beacon*

Distance	10 miles (16km)
Map	OS Explorer 122 Brighton & Hove 1:25,000
Start	Below Hassocks Railway Station on B2116 (TQ 305 155)
Access	By rail on the London to Brighton line; by bus from Burgess Hill. The town is located east of A273 between Haywards Heath and Brighton.
Parking	Public car parks in Hassocks, at the Clayton Windmills (TQ 303 135) and by Ditchling Beacon (TQ 333 131)
Refreshments	Pubs, cafés and shops in Hassocks

This splendid figure-of-eight walk visits the well-known Clayton Windmills and the site of an Iron Age fort at Ditchling Beacon. It also explores the folding downland that edges towards Brighton, and rewards with a series of vast panoramic views across the patchwork Weald. It's a walk to enjoy and to savour long afterwards.

Below Hassocks station, a few paces east of the railway bridge which spans the B2116, two footpaths are sited close together, with a bus stop between them. Take the path nearest the bridge, climb a few steps then go straight ahead beside a fence. Before long it is joined by the alternative path. Pass alongside **Butcher's Wood** (owned by The Woodland Trust), then a meadow and beyond this, Lag Wood, ignoring alternative paths. ◄ Reaching the A273 bear left, cross the B2112, then maintain direction a very short distance until you reach Underhill Lane on the edge of **Clayton**.

After Lag Wood the two Clayton Windmills may be seen on the crest of the Downs ahead.

Nestling at the foot of the Downs, the tiny village of **Clayton** was recorded in the Domesday Book of 1086. The squat, shingle-spired church of St John the Baptist has a Norman doorway, a Saxon chancel arch, and

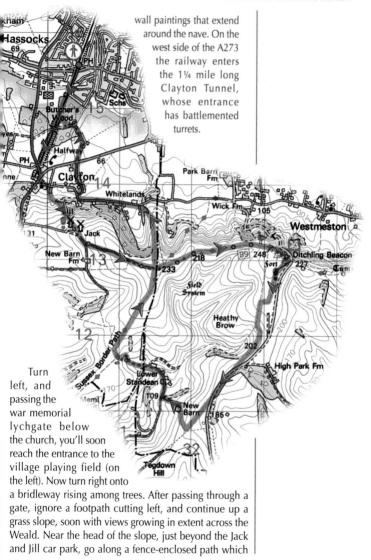

wall paintings that extend around the nave. On the west side of the A273 the railway enters the 1¼ mile long Clayton Tunnel, whose entrance has battlemented turrets.

Turn left, and passing the war memorial lychgate below the church, you'll soon reach the entrance to the village playing field (on the left). Now turn right onto a bridleway rising among trees. After passing through a gate, ignore a footpath cutting left, and continue up a grass slope, soon with views growing in extent across the Weald. Near the head of the slope, just beyond the Jack and Jill car park, go along a fence-enclosed path which

95

Jill, one of the two Clayton windmills

skirts the left-hand side of the **Clayton Windmills** and brings you onto a track where you turn left.

> The **Clayton Windmills** stand almost side by side on an imposing site high on the Downs above Clayton village. The black tower-mill known as Jack was built in 1866, but Jill, the white-painted post-mill, was brought here from Patcham near Brighton in 1821, hauled by a team of oxen. Cared for by The Jack and Jill Windmill Society, Jill, a working corn mill until 1909, is usually open to the public from 2-5pm on Sundays and Bank Holidays, May to September. Jack is privately owned with no public access.

When the track forks take the left branch, following the South Downs Way, initially heading southeast. ▶ A few paces before reaching the second gate along the track, note the large four-way Keymer signpost on the left – on the homeward leg of the walk the route descends the steep slope below the post (TQ 315 128). The SDW veers round to a northeasterly direction and soon passes Burnthouse Pond, a fence-enclosed dew pond beside a mass of gorse bushes. No longer a track the SDW path now continues past a second dew pond (this one on the right) with beautiful views in all directions.

Big open views reveal the sea far to the right beyond Brighton.

About a mile beyond Burnthouse Pond you come to the bushy mound of Ditchling Beacon (TQ 332 131).

Shortly before reaching a car park, there's another path on the right. Go up the slope and through a gate where this footpath takes you past bushes and between open fields heading south with expansive views left, to the eastern Downs.

Alternative
An alternative footpath breaks to the right immediately before the **Ditchling Beacon mound**, and a few paces beyond a trig point (seen on the right on the eastern side of the bushes).

Dew ponds, like this one near Ditchling Beacon, provide an important water supply for animals grazing the otherwise dry South Downs

The site of an Iron Age hillfort, at 813ft (248m) **Ditchling Beacon** is the highest of the Sussex Downs, described by the Victorian nature writer Richard Jeffries (in *Nature near London*), as 'the nearest and most accessible of the southern Alps from London'. In the past a beacon placed here would be lit to warn of an invasion, for it is said that its fire would be seen from Seaford in the east, and also from as far away as the North Downs.

At the end of the first field section, turn right on a farm track which soon reaches a gate and a broad crossing path – the alternative route from Ditchling Beacon. Bear left and walk down the slope to another gate, where the way forks. Take the left branch to contour round the east slope of downland above the lovely North Bottom. ◀ The path leads to a gate through which you soon come to the Ditchling Road at what is known as Highpark Corner (TQ 326 116).

This downland slope is yellow with cowslips in springtime.

Cross the road with care, aiming half-right to a continuing footpath inside a narrow woodland. At the end of this do not exit through a gate, but veer right to cross the road once more (again with care). Over a stile cross a meadow half-left to another stile in the boundary fence. Maintain direction across another open meadow above the large grey **New Barn**. On reaching the far side, turn right and walk down a track which takes you round the end of the barn and between fields to Wonderhill Plantation. At a crossing farm road/track turn right.

The track curves below a house and past the rather untidy farm of **Lower Standean**. Ignore alternative paths and remain on the track as it rises between fields, then swings round a small flint-and-brick barn. Go through a gate, turn left and follow the boundary of an open meadow as far as a marker post on the left. Now turn right and walk straight across the meadow on a faint grass trail used by the **Sussex Border Path**. On the far side go through a gate by gorse bushes and into the next large meadow.

The Sussex Border Path actually angles half-right across this downland meadow, but it may be that the only 'path' that is evident on the ground strikes more or less straight ahead, soon with a sighting of the Clayton Windmills ahead to the left and a fine view west through the Pyecombe gap. Should you reach the crossing track of the South Downs Way without first coming to a fence (as you would if you followed the correct line of the SBP), turn right for a few paces to reach the Keymer post. If, however, you kept to the correct line of the Sussex Border Path, turn left on reaching the boundary fence and follow this to the track of the SDW which you meet with the Keymer post directly ahead (TQ 315 128).

Passing the tall oak post on your right, descend the slope ahead on a clear path between gorse bushes, with exquisite views of the Weald ahead, with Hassocks and Keymer below, a solitary white windmill standing just beyond Keymer, and dramatic mounds and hollows to the right of the path. Two thirds of the way down the slope, take the left branch when it forks and you will come onto Underhill Lane between Clayton and Westmeston. Turn left and wander along the lane at the foot of the Downs for a little over ½ mile (800m). Shortly after passing

Burnthouse Pond, the gorse-banked dew pond on the way to Ditchling Beacon

the Clayton sign, the lane bends to the right, then as it curves left, turn right on another narrow lane past several houses. The lane becomes a gravel drive. After the last house continue ahead on a lovely bridleway among trees, soon alongside a long, narrow pond.

Reaching the B2112 cross to a track/drive leading to a house named **Halfway**. After passing this the track curves left towards an isolated house (Woodbine) on the edge of **Butcher's Wood**. Immediately before a cattle grid, cross a stile on the left, then veer right up a grass slope, cross an open meadow to its far right-hand corner, and rejoin the outward footpath near the railway line. Turn right and follow this past Butcher's Wood all the way to the B2116 at Hassocks.

WALK 16

Devil's Dyke to Edburton Hill and Poynings

Distance	6½ miles (10.5km)
Map	OS Explorer 122 Brighton & Hove 1:25,000
Start	Devil's Dyke Hotel (TQ 258 111)
Access	By bus 77 (Brighton & Hove Bus Company) from Brighton (April to September). By the Devil's Dyke Road south of Poynings
Parking	Pay and display car park at the Devil's Dyke Hotel
Refreshments	Pubs at Devil's Dyke and in Poynings

Named after the narrow and steeply-walled dry valley that opens to the south of Poynings, the Iron Age fort of Devil's Dyke is one of the finest and most easily-accessible of all downland vantage points, with a minor road leading to its crown where there's a hotel and large car park. The precipitous north face of the escarpment looks down on Poynings, Fulking and the few buildings of Edburton, while to the south the Downs fold away to Brighton and the coast. Footpaths abound here, and it should be possible to create a number of rewarding circuits and tours. This is just one of them; a circular walk which begins by heading west along the downland crest to Edburton Hill, where it then descends into the low-lying Weald before linking several footpaths heading roughly eastward to Poynings. There you turn south to climb the flank of the Devil's Dyke back to your starting point.

From the Devil's Dyke Hotel take a narrow footpath heading southwest (left when facing the Weald) along the head of the escarpment. ▶ Go through a kissing gate and pass below a ruin, and before long come to a bridle gate on the edge of Fulking Escarpment. Now join the South Downs Way and wander ahead with the radio masts on Truleigh Hill seen nearly 2 miles (3.2km) away.

As you make progress, the SDW becomes a broad chalk and flint bridleway. Ignoring alternative paths cross **Perching Hill**, then descend into a dip below a line of

Fulking can be seen at the foot of the slope to your right.

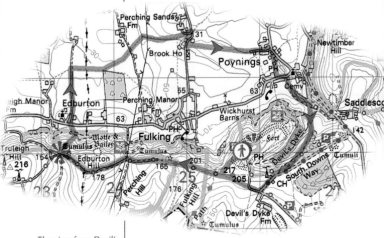

The view from Devil's Dyke looking west along the Fulking Escarpment

power cables where there's a crossing path (Southwick to the left, Fulking to the right). Keep ahead to loop round the left-hand side of **Edburton Hill**, after which you return

to the crest of the Downs, pass through a gate and turn hard right to leave the SDW. Go through a second gate where a sunken path begins its descent to Edburton.

The path soon becomes a 'shelf' angling northeastward down the escarpment with lovely views, the hillsides on either side yellow with cowslips in springtime. Near the foot of the slope the path cuts back to the left below a small wooded area, then goes through a gate on the right which leads to a narrow lane at Edburton (TQ 234 114). Cross directly ahead and walk along a drive. Passing Aburton Farmhouse continue along a path enclosed by fences then hedgerows for almost ½ mile (800m). On coming to a crossing path with a four-way signpost, turn right on a narrow bridleway.

At the end of the first field where the bridleway swings left, maintain direction over a plank footbridge and a stile, and continue ahead in a second field towards a corner of Perching Hovel Wood. Over a track and another plank footbridge, branch half-left across a third field aiming towards what appears to be its far left-hand corner. Come to a farm drive where a stile then gives access to the meadow opposite, across which you aim half-right to another farm drive, this one well to the left of Perching Sands Farm Cottages.

Cross another stile and maintain direction. On the far side of this field there's a stile next to a field gate, then over a stream wander along the right-hand edge of a meadow. On the far side continue among trees and bushes. When the path forks keep ahead (the right-hand option goes to Fulking). Passing more bushes the path brings you to a drive where you turn right, and in a few paces come onto a narrow lane at TQ 251 126. Turn right.

The lane curves right and left past houses, after which you cross a stile on the left next to a field gate. Walk slightly left ahead across a meadow to its far boundary and another stile. ▶ Over the stile enter an open field and maintain direction to yet another stile beside a field gate, then go slightly left ahead, cross a stream onto a track, and follow this as far as the northernmost group of

The Devil's Dyke can be clearly seen from here.

houses of **Poynings**, passing along the way a pond and a waste water treatment works.

A few paces before reaching Poynings Road, turn right on a footpath alongside a fence. At a crossing path turn right to pass a paddock, then between banks of trees (wild garlic in springtime) eventually arrive beside The Royal Oak pub in Poynings.

Turn left along a raised footpath above the road. When this slopes down to road level, cross to the right and walk down the side of a garage into a meadow. Follow the left-hand boundary as far as a stile. Over this continue round the edge of a pond, then by way of more stiles come to a crossing path where you turn right into a very narrow tree-crowded valley. Over a stream the path rises and eventually emerges from the trees at the entrance to the dry valley of **Devil's Dyke**.

The deep, dry valley of Devil's Dyke

The dry valley of the **Devil's Dyke** is said to be the largest single coombe of chalk karst in Britain. The National Trust owns much of the surrounding area, which covers

183 acres of downland. The scrub-covered slopes provide a habitat for the Scarce Forester moth and Adonis Blue butterfly, while the native flora includes several species of orchid, as well as cowslip, wild thyme, horseshoe vetch and birdsfoot trefoil.

Edburton's church stands at the foot of the Downs

One path strikes directly through the valley, but we take the alternative route branching slightly left, to angle up and across the southeast slope, with fine views for much of the way. At the head of the slope bear right along the South Downs Way and follow this to a gate. Through this cross the Devil's Dyke access road and continue on the SDW across open downland towards the Truleigh Hill radio masts. On coming to the bridle gate with a narrow path coming from the right, leave the South Downs Way and return to the Devil's Dyke Hotel along the alternative path.

WALK 17

Devil's Dyke to Mile Oak Barn and Edburton Hill

Distance	6½ miles (10.5km)
Map	OS Explorer 122 Brighton & Hove 1:25,000
Start	Devil's Dyke Hotel (TQ 258 111)
Access	By bus 77 (Brighton & Hove Bus Company) from Brighton (April to September). By the Devil's Dyke Road south of Poynings
Parking	Pay and display car park at the Devil's Dyke Hotel
Refreshments	Pub at Devil's Dyke

The second of our walks from the popular Devil's Dyke viewpoint, this one heads south away from the escarpment with a sea view for the first half, before returning to the downland edge by way of a charming little valley caught in a fold of the Downs. This is a very pleasant, fairly undemanding walk, with good views despite the presence of power lines for much of the way.

The chimneys of the Portslade power station are a major landmark.

The start is identical to that of Walk 16, for it takes the narrow footpath heading left opposite the Devil's Dyke Hotel. Going through a kissing gate on the edge of the escarpment, continue ahead as far as a bridle gate where the route of the South Downs Way enters the National Trust land of Fulking Escarpment. Through the gate ignore the SDW and branch half-left to cross the open downland of **Fulking Hill**, with the buildings of Brighton and Portslade seen ahead on the coast. ◀ On the far side of the large downland meadow come to a second bridle gate in a fence running diagonally across the route. Through the gate wander straight ahead, now with a fence on your left and a large arable field stretching off to the right. The path eventually becomes a track, and immediately after passing beneath power lines, you turn right on another track cutting between arable fields (TQ 249 092). On reaching a pylon the track curves sharply to the left and takes you along the west side of Cockroost Hill. On a gradual descent of the hill note Mile Oak dew pond on the right, shortly after which the track forks.

Take the right branch, go through a bridle gate and continue down the slope to Mile Oak Barn. At the foot of the slope, immediately before the barn, go through another gate and turn right on a broad crossing track. This soon curves right, heading north with pylons and over-head power lines making an unwelcome intrusion across the landscape. Passing beneath the cables the track then veers left along Hazelholt Bottom before it forks. Take the right branch between hedges running parallel with the power lines for a while, with Truleigh Hill Barn seen ahead on the skyline.

On drawing level with a brick barn, go through a gate into a sloping downland meadow and slant half-left uphill – during research a helpful blue waymark had been painted on the side of a water trough to indicate the way. Curving round the hill you eventually come to yet another gate in a fence, through which you turn right into a charming little valley whose right flank is dotted with scrub. As the way progresses towards the head of the valley it follows a fence-line, and brings you to the crossing track of the South Downs Way in a saddle between **Edburton Hill** and Truleigh Hill.

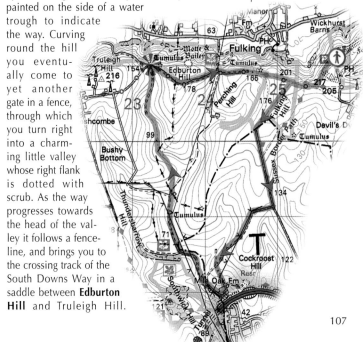

Curving round Edburton Hill, this flint and chalk track takes the walk back to the Devil's Dyke

Although our route turns right here, it is worth walking ahead a few paces to enjoy a glorious view into the Weald, with the Downs making a long curving line to the right. Return to Devil's Dyke by following the flint and chalk track of the South Downs Way round Edburton Hill, then dropping into a dip below power lines, after which you cross **Perching Hill** with Fulking seen below. After leaving Fulking Escarpment through a bridle gate, the SDW track becomes a narrow path. Leave it here and branch left along the same path on which the walk began. This leads directly back to the Devil's Dyke Hotel and car park.

WALK 18

Wiston to No Man's Land

Distance	6½ miles (10.5km)
Map	OS Explorer 121 Arundel & Pulborough 1:25,000
Start	Chanctonbury Car Park (TQ 145 124)
Access	Via Chanctonbury Ring Road, off A283, 1½ miles east of Washington
Parking	At Chanctonbury Car Park and Picnic Site
Refreshments	None

East of Chanctonbury Ring a mix of large arable fields, downland pasture and strips of woodland bring variety to the South Downs, and while the many open panoramic views include the sea, between Washington and Steyning the north-facing slopes bear a dense cover of trees that restrict views out over the Weald. On this walk we begin by heading roughly eastward along the foot of the Downs, passing Wiston House on the way, before making a steady ascent through woodland to gain a surprise view from Steyning Round Hill. We then follow the route of the Monarch's Way to the hollow of No Man's Land, then tour the hills north of Cissbury Ring on the way back to the start.

Leaving the car park walk along the lane towards the Downs, then take the first turning on the left – a track which soon passes the buildings of **Great Barn Farm**, one of which is raised upon staddle stones. Beyond the farm buildings the track continues (it can be muddy at times) heading east, and after crossing a couple of stiles next to field gates, it becomes a narrow surfaced lane, across which there's a footbridge shortly before you can see the rather austere grey mansion of **Wiston House** to the left.

In the 18th century, **Wiston House** was home to Charles Goring, the man who, in 1760, planted the beech grove of Chanctonbury Ring that is such a distinctive feature of this part of the South Downs.

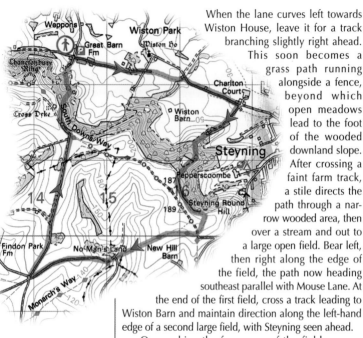

When the lane curves left towards Wiston House, leave it for a track branching slightly right ahead. This soon becomes a grass path running alongside a fence, beyond which open meadows lead to the foot of the wooded downland slope. After crossing a faint farm track, a stile directs the path through a narrow wooded area, then over a stream and out to a large open field. Bear left, then right along the edge of the field, the path now heading southeast parallel with Mouse Lane. At the end of the first field, cross a track leading to Wiston Barn and maintain direction along the left-hand edge of a second large field, with Steyning seen ahead.

On reaching the far corner of the field, cross a stile, go down some steps onto a sunken track, and turn right (TQ 168 117). The track narrows to a footpath as it rises gently alongside a woodland shaw, then enters the woods that clothe the steepening slope. After a few paces the bridleway forks. It's perfectly feasible to walk ahead on the left-hand option, but the official way branches right, then left (near a small flint-walled ruin) and rejoins the direct route. Continue ahead up the slope ignoring alternative paths branching left and right, until you come to a fork marked by an oak post. Both options are bridleways, but we take the left branch, the more narrow of the two.

The gradient steepens, then eases, and the bridleway is joined by a footpath rising from Steyning. Still climbing you soon approach the head of the slope to be

joined by another path, this one entering from the right. The way veers left and, still among trees, eases along the head of the steep slope, but just below the open Downs, before emerging to a junction with a seat exploiting a lovely view over Steyning and Bramber, and the long curving line of the eastern Downs stretching into the distance (TQ 164 103).

Seen from a seat at a junction of paths, Steyning lies at the foot of the Downs

Turn right and follow a path alongside a fence with big views growing in extent as you progress, and eventually come to crossing tracks. The South Downs Way crosses our route at this point. Walk straight ahead onto a gravel path between fences. This is part of The Monarch's Way. On the left stands a touching memorial to Sussex farmer, Walter Langmead, whose ashes were laid to rest here, along with those of his wife 'on his cherished Downs'.

The Monarch's Way is a route of 615 miles (990km) which follows the trail of Charles II on his escape following defeat in the Battle of Worcester in 1651. The route begins in Worcester and makes a long circuitous journey ending in Shoreham.

The path goes between large arable fields, then down a slope to a crossing track in a scrubby area known as **No Man's Land**. Here The Monarch's Way footpath goes ahead among bushes. We leave it here and take a narrow parallel path, also between bushes which, during research, were rather overgrown.

Alternative
The right-hand track climbing the slope above **No Man's Land** leads into our route, so it could be taken as an alternative to going through the bushes.

The Monarch's Way is one of several long distance routes to cross the South Downs

112

Emerging from the bushes the path curves right and soon joins the track mentioned above. Continue uphill heading west between more large arable fields, with the broad sprawling hill of Cissbury Ring (see Walk 19) seen to the south, with the English Channel beyond.

On coming to a major junction of tracks turn sharply to the right (red waymark) on a chalk track which forks after a few paces. Take the right branch, in effect straight ahead. Rising across the Downs it passes through a brief woodland, shortly after which it forks again. Continue ahead, ignoring the left branch. Nearing the crest of the Downs with expansive views (especially fine looking back), come to yet another fork. Take the left branch ahead and shortly after, the crown of trees that mark Chanctonbury Ring (see Walk 20) comes into view.

A few paces beyond the crest of the Downs come to a four-way junction, where the South Downs Way crosses our route. Keep ahead on a bridleway descending through Chalkpit Wood; the track is known as Wiston Bostal. The woods are delightful, and near the foot of the slope a huge beech tree can be seen to the right of the path with an intricate web of roots revealed where the slope below has been washed away. Out of the woods you come to the head of Chanctonbury Ring Road, then wander ahead to the car park where the walk began.

WALK 19

Findon to Cissbury Ring

Distance	7 miles (11km)
Map	OS Explorer 121 Arundel & Pulborough 1:25,000
Start	The Square, Findon (TQ 122 088)
Access	By bus: services from Worthing and Midhurst. Findon is located about 4 miles north of Worthing, off the A24
Parking	Limited parking in The Square at the bottom of Stable Lane (TQ 122 088); there is also small car park below Cissbury Ring (TQ 139 085)
Refreshments	Pubs, shop and café in Findon

Immediately to the east of Findon, the downland slopes are used for exercising racehorses, but spreading farther away the sprawling open country offers a mixture of arable and pastureland. Between Chanctonbury Ring and Cissbury Ring it's largely treeless, with hills folding into waterless valleys. Footpaths, bridleways and farm tracks strike across the landscape, the only meagre shade on hot summer days being cast by low-growing scrub. But the huge Iron Age hillfort of Cissbury Ring (one of the largest in the country) is circled by trees as well as scrub. This ancient site, with its historic flint mines, testifies to man's occupation of the South Downs for more than 5000 years and is the focus of this walk.

From the crossroads in the heart of Findon, opposite two pubs (the Gunn Inn and Village House), walk along The Square and bear left into the residential street of Stable Lane. This rises gently to the upper end of the village where the lane ends. A private drive to Gallops Farm goes directly ahead, while we follow a track on the right which leads onto the crest of the Downs.

About a third of a mile from the end of Stable Lane, a lone house stands back on the left as the last habitation on the walk before the return to Findon. Half a mile beyond this come to crosstracks at TQ 139 095. The broad chalk path on the left goes to Chanctonbury Ring, that on the right goes to Cissbury Ring. We continue directly ahead on a slightly more narrow track than that used thus far.

An immense **panorama** unfolds. Far ahead the radio masts on Truleigh Hill are clearly evident; off to the right the English Channel glistens and glimmers in the sunshine. In summer larks rise to become tiny specks in the sky; their unmistakable trilling sound being the quintessential song of downland. In winter, though, the land is stark and grey, often with arctic-like winds scouring across the open countryside.

The track slopes downhill towards the hollow of No Man's Land, and forks on the way. Whilst it is feasible to keep to the main track, a waymark post directs the route to branch right. This soon enters scrub and, curving left, takes you down into **No Man's Land**, where there's a junction of paths and tracks. Keep ahead for a few paces, then turn right on a bridleway between fences. This soon goes between two parallel lines of scrub-like trees through a narrow valley known as Stump Bottom, eventually reaching a crossing track where you bear right through a bridle gate at TQ 152 083.

Fences and a few bushes now lead the way through **Canada Bottom** with the earth-works of Cissbury Ring rising above to the left.

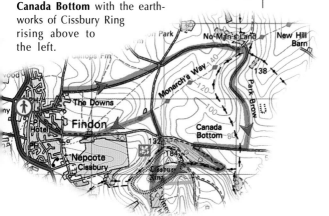

There are blackberries here in late summer. About 40 yards after a solitary barn, go through a gate on the left and cut back along a path at the bottom edge of National Trust land. On reaching a second gate, do not go through it, but instead turn sharp right on a path rising up a slope of scrub.

Almost at the head of the slope go through the second gate on the left, then bear right to a kissing gate giving access to the earthen ramparts of **Cissbury Ring**. A path cuts through these on the way to a trig point, but the suggestion here is to bear left inside the ramparts to

Like many important sites on the South Downs, Cissbury Ring is in the care of the National Trust

CISSBURY RING

Covering no less than 65 acres, Cissbury Ring is the largest and most impressive of the many earthworks that punctuate the South Downs. There are two clearly defined ramparts of this Iron Age hillfort, which dates from about 300 to 59BC, and it has been estimated that about 60,000 tons of chalk had to be dug from the ditch in order to build them. Long before the hillfort was created, flint mining was carried out here during the New Stone Age (4300–3500BC), and shafts up to 40ft (12m) deep, leading to galleries, have been discovered here. Even a quick examination of the site reveals a whole series of mounds and depressions which tell of this mining activity, and would suggest that Cissbury was one of southern England's foremost flint mining sites.

Before the Roman occupation, Cissbury Ring was abandoned as a fortification, but it was reoccupied and fortified once more at the end of the Roman period, presumably as a defence against the Saxons.

make a partial circuit of this ancient site. Views are outstanding in all directions from the outer ramparts, with Beachy Head in one direction, the Isle of Wight and the spire of Chichester Cathedral in another. On coming to the southernmost part, turn right on a crossing path. Passing a group of nicely shaped oak trees walk ahead towards some gorse bushes. When the path forks, take the left branch ahead which brings you to the trig point at 603ft (184m). Bear left and walk down the slope to a tree-shaded seat with a wonderful panoramic view, then turn left for a short distance until coming to some steps descending on the right. These lead to a footpath which leaves Cissbury Ring and comes to a small unmade car park at the head of a narrow lane (TQ 139 085).

Walk through the car park and along a continuing track between large fields. At the end of the first field

The track that leads to No Man's Land

section turn left along a narrow bridleway adopted by the long distance Monarch's Way. The windmill at High Salvington above Worthing is just visible to the south-west, with the sea beyond that. The fence-enclosed bridleway descends to a lane where you bear right, soon passing alongside Nepcote Green. On coming to a crossing lane keep ahead along Nepcote Lane, which leads directly to The Square in Findon and the end of the walk.

WALK 20

Washington to Chanctonbury Ring

Distance	4¾ miles (7.5km)
Map	OS Explorer 121 Arundel & Pulborough 1:25,000
Start	Washington car park (TQ 120 120)
Access	By bus from Midhurst, and Worthing. Washington lies south of the A24/A283 Junction
Parking	Washington car park on the South Downs Way
Refreshments	Pub in Washington

One of the best-known features of the Sussex Downs is the prominent crown of trees on Chanctonbury Ring, the 4-acre site of an Iron Age hillfort southeast of Washington. From either side the downland crest affords magnificent views, so its popularity is assured. This rectangular walk makes the best of those views, but begins by first skirting the foot of the steep slope.

At the entrance to the car park at the foot of the Downs a little east of the A24, head north along a track above the former main road. When it curves right, continue ahead on what is a private drive but public footpath, serving a few houses. On coming to a multi-junction of tracks cut back to the left to descend round a bend among trees, and eventually come onto London Road on the outskirts of Washington village. The second turning on the left is The Street, and about 50 yards beyond it there's a stile on the right at TQ 123 127.

Across the stile footpath takes you over a plank footbridge, up a flight of steps and into a field. Wander along the left-hand edge of this field, and eventually come onto a track. Continue into a second field by Tilley's Farm and maintain direction until, about 100 yards from the far end, a footpath sign directs the route half-right to a stile leading into a third field. Once again maintain direction,

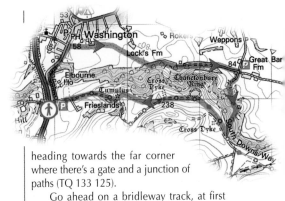

heading towards the far corner where there's a gate and a junction of paths (TQ 133 125).

Go ahead on a bridleway track, at first edging the woods of Combe Holt, then rising a little among trees before sloping down again to pass alongside the old corrugated Owlscroft Barn, with its rust-red roof. The track continues along the lower edge of the woods: it's heavily rutted and very muddy at times. On

The prominent tree-crowned summit of Chanctonbury Ring

emerging from the woods you gain long views of the Downs stretching far ahead beyond the Adur's breach at Steyning, and eventually come onto Chanctonbury Ring Road by the side of Malthouse Cottage. Turn right. ▶ Within a few paces the lane ends and a track continues directly ahead, passing a reservoir on the right. The track soon begins to climb the wooded slope, winding past a lovely group of beech trees, one of whose roots have been exposed where the chalky soil has been washed away. The track (a bridleway) is known as Wiston Bostal and it makes a steady ascent of Chalkpit Wood, emerging to a four-way crossing track beside a charming little fence-enclosed flower meadow at TQ 144 114. Turn right and wander westward along the broad track of the South Downs Way, rising gently to gain a first sighting of **Chanctonbury Ring** ahead.

Chanctonbury Car Park is about 100 yards down the lane to the left.

CHANCTONBURY RING

Chanctonbury Ring is the site of an Iron Age hillfort which contained a Romano-Celtic temple of the third or fourth centuries. It is assumed that there were links with nearby Cissbury Ring (see Walk 19), another hillfort of the same period found across the Downs to the south. The clump of beech and sycamores that adorns the site was planted in 1760 by Charles Goring of Wiston House (see Walk 18) who, during the first few months, made regular visits carrying water up the steep slope (no doubt it was his workmen who did the carrying) until the young trees were established. During the 'hurricane' that wreaked havoc across the southern counties on 16 October 1987, many of the trees were uprooted, but their replacements are now making their presence felt.

Gaining the crest of the Downs on the approach to Chanctonbury Ring a splendid view is gained across the Weald, as there is on the western side of the crown of trees. Pass along the left-hand (south) side of the trees below a trig point, and remain on the South Downs Way until it goes through a gate with a cattle grid. Now leave the SDW and bear right to pass through another gate by Chanctonbury Dew Pond at TQ 133 120.

The humps and hollows below Chanctonbury Ring

The small scoop of **Chanctonbury Dew Pond** was constructed in 1870 and restored 100 years later by the Society of Sussex Downsmen. From the rim of this Site of Special Scientific Interest another splendid panoramic view includes Cissbury Ring to the south, the Weald below and out to the north, with the South Downs reaching west towards unseen Amberley. The ugly scar of a huge sand quarry outside Washington is the only jarring intrusion to disturb the harmony of the view.

There are masses of cowslips here in springtime.

Pass to the left of the dew pond and angle across the downland crest heading west, then descend the slope (with some of the loveliest views of the walk) to a gate in the lower boundary fence. ◄ Through this the trail weaves among humps and hollows before rejoining the South Downs Way, which has made a curious dog-leg since we left it near the dew pond. Now follow this downhill to Washington car park.

WALK 21
Washington to Kithurst Hill

Distance	7½ miles (12km)
Map	OS Explorer 121 Arundel & Pulborough 1:25,000
Start	The Street, Washington (TQ 122 127)
Access	By bus: from Midhurst, Pulborough and Worthing. Washington lies south of the A24/A283 junction
Parking	Limited parking north of Washington (TQ 122 132); at foot of South Downs Way (TQ 120 120); above Storrington (TQ 071 125) and at Chantry Post (TQ 087 119)
Refreshments	Pub in Washington

West of the A24 the Downs give the impression of a broader range of hills than those further east. This walk begins by heading west below the Downs, but after passing Sullington church it curves up onto the escarpment between Chantry Hill and Kithurst Hill, soon to gain vast panoramic views that seem to grow better with each step. A hilltop car park above Storrington is the turning point, with a return to Washington being made along the route of the South Downs Way.

A short distance southwest of the Frankland Arms pub in Washington, walk along The Street to pass a number of attractive cottages on the way to the Parish Church of St Mary's. Beyond the church a road bridge takes you over the A24. When it forks take the right branch, a stony track/drive leading to Rowdell House. Immediately before the track bends to the right by the house, leave it for a bridleway on the left used by the South Downs Way. After a few paces bear right between laurel bushes, then alongside a fence, round a garden boundary and into a field. Walk ahead between fields until you come to **Barns Farm** at TQ 104 130.

Through a gate the fence enclosed bridleway makes a dog-leg round the farm, then forks. Take the left branch among trees, go through a gate and into a meadow. Keep to the right-hand edge of this meadow, and on reaching the far side by some barns veer right, then left by St Mary's Church, Sullington. A track goes between the church and a barn, and after passing a house, keep ahead along the edge of another meadow with lovely views across the Weald. Ahead to the left a chalk path can be seen cutting up the slope of Chantry Hill; this will soon be taken by our route.

At the end of the meadow the way angles left down a woodland slope, then through a gate turns right alongside Waterfall Cottage and onto a narrow lane. Turn left, and moments later pass the little waterfall after which the cottage is named. Shortly afterwards come to two attractive ponds at the entrance to Chantry Mere. Now turn right on a track leading to farm buildings where you go through a gate and walk up a gently sloping meadow with a view left into a downland coombe.

Through another gate pass along the edge of woodland, then go left through yet another gate where the path forks. Take the left branch to climb a slope, still alongside the wood. As you gain height the path becomes more prominent. Above the trees walk up a flower-starred hillside from which you gain splendid views, not only of the Downs stretching beyond Chanctonbury Ring, but of the heavily wooded Weald north of Storrington.

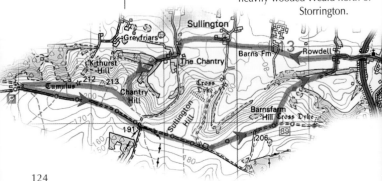

Arriving at a path junction on Chantry Hill, a fine view is gained into the Weald

Join another bridleway rising from the right and continue towards the head of **Chantry Hill** to join a crossing path where you turn right. ▶

Wonderful views again threaten to delay progress, but add greatly to the pleasures of the walk.

Shortcut

On coming to a bridle gate a few paces from the trig point on **Kithurst Hill** (699ft: 213m), note that a path goes off to the left which links with the South Downs Way and could be used to shortcut our walk by 1½ miles (2.4km).

Unless you wish to do this shortcut, keep ahead, now with the English Channel seen to the left and the outline of the Isle of Wight to the southwest.

After passing another crossing bridle path (a second opportunity to shortcut the walk by taking the left-hand option) the way goes through a tunnel of trees and bushes with a tangle of honeysuckle and wild clematis, then alongside a beautiful wild flower meadow. At the end of this you arrive at the Kithurst Hill car park above Storrington at TQ 071 125. Go through a gate on the left onto the crossing track of the South Downs Way and turn left; in effect now walking roughly parallel with the previous bridleway.

The SDW track leads mostly between arable fields for a little over a mile. You then arrive at the Chantry Post car park at TQ 087 119. Keep ahead to cross the meadowland of **Sullington Hill** until the way forks by a barn. Remain on the South Downs Way, which takes the left branch onto **Barnsfarm Hill**. There you gain yet more lovely views, this time including Chanctonbury Ring and Cissbury Ring (see Walks 19 and 20). About 250 yards after passing through a bridle gate the track forks once more. Both options are taken by the SDW, but we branch left through a field and over the brow of the hill. A few paces to the right, note an information board and a seat made from a tree trunk. From here yet another glorious panoramic view may be enjoyed.

The Chantry Post marks a major crossways on the Downs

The continuing way descends the slope and curves right to the bottom of a meadow, where you branch left into some trees and come onto a very narrow surfaced track. This becomes a sunken lane between banks of wild garlic in springtime. Emerging from the woodland pass a couple of houses, and when the lane curves right walk directly ahead among more trees, then come onto a crossing track by Rowdell House. Turn right and follow this track and lane (the outward route) back to Washington.

WALK 22

Chantry Post to Myrtle Grove Farm

Distance	7 miles (11km)
Map	OS Explorer 121 Arundel & Pulborough 1:25,000
Start	Chantry Post car park above Storrington (TQ 087 119)
Access	Via Chantry Lane off A283 ½ mile east of Storrington
Parking	Chantry Post car park at the head of Chantry Lane
Refreshments	None on route

This is a very fine circular walk which crosses downland meadows, cuts through large arable fields and exploits numerous enchanting vistas. Taking bridleways and tracks, there are neither stiles nor steep slopes on this walk. It's a route for idling along, a walk loud with the song of skylarks and bright with poppies, but note that there are very few trees to provide shade on a bright summer's day, and as there are no refreshment facilities along the way you should remember to pack a picnic lunch and plenty of liquids.

At the Chantry Post take the track used by the South Downs Way heading east towards Washington. Wandering across the grassland of **Sullington Hill**, approach a grey barn and, a few paces before this, leave the SDW and walk along the right-hand side of the barn, then keep ahead alongside a fence. Reaching the woods of Highden Beeches, come onto a track which skirts the right-hand edge of the woods, then joins another track along which you curve right.

Wandering southeastward now, with big sweeping views that include Cissbury Ring, the way progresses without making any physical demands. When the track forks keep ahead through a gate where you come onto a surfaced track/drive. ▶ Easy walking eventually leads to a crossing track which serves New Barn off to the right, and **Muntham Farm** to the left. Keep ahead, now on a cart track

Here the left-hand bank is full of poppies in early summer.

127

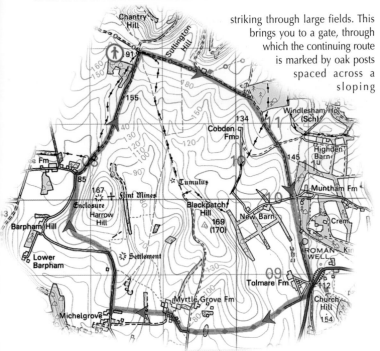

striking through large fields. This brings you to a gate, through which the continuing route is marked by oak posts spaced across a sloping

meadow. On the far side of this go through another gate and maintain direction on a narrow bridleway squeezed between bushes, leading to another track junction a few paces before reaching the A280 at TQ 110 089.

Turn right onto a farm drive which leads to **Tolmare Farm**, but almost immediately fork left along a bridleway adopted by the Monarch's Way. With farm buildings off to the right the hedge-lined cart track slopes downhill, then rises to large open fields guided by fences. Now, with neither tree nor hedgerow to offer shade, the way crosses the north side of a lovely valley through which the A280 curves below the steep slope of the south flank. ◄

The fencing ends at a gate, beyond which you continue through the middle of another large open field, with

Longfurlong Barn can be seen below in the valley bottom, while the spire of Patching church protrudes above trees to the southwest.

the buildings of Longfurlong Farm ahead to the right. After this go through a gateway and keep ahead on the left-hand side of the next field, to reach a farm drive. Turn left, then right on another drive leading to **Myrtle Grove Farm**. Ignore alternatives and follow the drive into the farmyard, where you bear left in front of the farm estate office, then follow a bridleway along the left-hand side of the house and on between fences. This eventually leads to a barn with a flintstone wall extending beyond it, where a track takes the route to a crossing narrow lane at TQ 083 085.

The Monarch's Way goes left, but we turn right and walk uphill on what is, in fact, a drive leading to the secluded buildings of Lee Farm. As you progress views grow in extent all around. When the drive curves left, leave it for a gate on the right next to a stile. Through the gate a bridleway slices through another large sloping field parallel with a line of power cables. Curving round the flank of **Harrow Hill** go through yet another gate and slope gently down a grassy hillside towards **Lee Farm**. This is one of the most attractive sections of the walk, with glorious views to enjoy: a chequerboard pattern of fields ahead, a gentle valley to the left backed by Barpham Hill (see Walk 25).

At the far left-hand corner of the meadow near a large barn, go through a gate, then turn right through another gate and follow a track as it curves left, rising through a second downland meadow. At the top of this a bridle gate takes the continuing track through more open fields and finally back to the car park by the Chantry Post.

Towards the end of the walk, the way approaches remote Lee Farm

WALK 23

Storrington to Parham Park and Rackham Hill

Distance	7½ miles (12km)
Map	OS Explorer 121 Arundel & Pulborough 1:25,000
Start	Amberley Road, Storrington (TQ 085 144)
Access	By bus: from Pulborough, Amberley and Washington. By road: Storrington is on the A283 about 2 miles west of Washington
Parking	Pay and display parking at junction of A283/B2139 (TQ 085 144): also on Kithurst Hill above Storrington (TQ 071 125)
Refreshments	Pubs and cafés in Storrington, pub in Cootham

West of Storrington, Parham Deer Park, with its great mansion, magnificent oak trees and long pond graced with lily pads, forms a prominent feature of this walk. The well-drained, low-lying Amberley Wild Brooks is another, for the route skirts this flat expanse of grass and reed before mounting the steep north slope of Rackham Hill and heading east along the crest of the Downs towards Kithurst Hill, visited on Walk 21. It's an interesting, very varied walk that is particularly rich in wild flowers and birdsong in spring and early summer.

From the A283/B2139 junction in Storrington, walk along Amberley Road for about 500 yards to where the road makes a gentle bend to the left. Now take an enclosed footpath on the right by the entrance to Cobb Cottage. This crosses a narrow road, continues along the back of several houses and over a footbridge. Beyond this a bridle gate leads into a field, across which you angle towards the left-hand side of a white house. Through another gate, walk along a drive as far as the A283 beside Cootham Village Hall (TQ 074 145). ◄

The Crown Inn stands a short distance to the right.

Turn left and walk alongside the road for about 250 yards, passing the entrance to the Southdown Gliding Club.

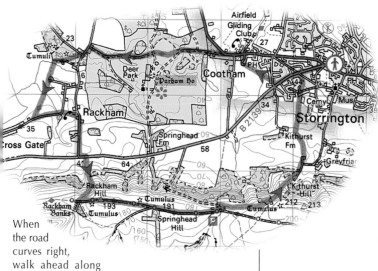

When the road curves right, walk ahead along a drive into **Parham Park**, which you enter at Douglas's Lodge. When the drive curves left take a grass path running parallel with it on the right. This leads north of Parham House which can be seen to the left (along

A partial view of Parham House is gained from the walk through its park

with the dovecote) with the South Downs as a backdrop. At a junction of drives continue ahead, soon passing alongside walls that surround the garden, then past a long pond, and finally out of the park by West Lodges at TQ 052 146. Turn left along Rackham Street.

PARHAM PARK

Parham Park and gardens cover an area of about 340 acres (137 hectares), and some of the magnificent specimen oak trees seen on the walk are more than 500 years old. There are also fine lime trees – note the mistletoe growing on them. Fallow deer have roamed the parkland since at least 1628, and now number about 350. The estate was formerly owned by the Abbey of Westminster, but following the dissolution of the monasteries in 1540 Henry VIII gave Parham House to a London mercer named Robert Palmer. The present house was built of local stone in 1577 by his son Thomas, who sailed with Francis Drake, but the eye-catching dovecote dates from the 18th century. The name Parham is an old one, and is said to mean 'the pear tree settlement', but the estate is better known today for the golden pippin apple which is thought to have originated here in 1629. The house and gardens are open on set days (afternoons only) April–September: **www.parhaminsussex.co.uk**.

Soon reach a junction of lanes, bear right along Greatham Road, and after a few paces enter woods on the left to follow a narrow path. At first predominantly holly and oak, as you wander through the woods so the variety of species includes beech, birch and ash. Coming to the edge of the woodland bear right to pass Pine Cottage, and continue along a footpath as far as the woodland corner. Now cross a footbridge on the left to head south alongside a fence bordering the expanse of Amberley Wild Brooks.

Over a stile pass between a house and a building shown on the 1:25,000 map as Rackham Mill, then enter another woodland. Out of the trees soon enter a meadow which you cross half-right ahead to a footbridge, then ahead to a field where the footpath aims for the far right-hand corner. Go through a gap onto a lane and turn left (TQ 044 136). When it makes a sharp left-hand bend, leave the lane, cross a stile on the right and walk across a sloping meadow. Over the brow aim for a house. A stile to the right of this leads the continuing path alongside the garden boundary and out to Rackham Street once more. Turn right, and pass a pretty thatched cottage on the way to the B2139.

Turn left for about 80 yards, then go through a gate on the right onto a bridleway which soon takes you through a small woodland and up the steepening slope of Rackham Hill. This downland slope is a riot of wild flowers in early summer, and as it curves to the right, expansive views reveal Amberley Wild Brooks below, the curling River Arun, and the long march of the Downs beyond Bignor Hill. At the head of the slope go through another gate onto the track of the South Downs Way and turn left.

Follow the SDW over **Rackham Hill**, then the wooded **Springhead Hill** and, almost 1½ miles after coming onto the Downs, you will arrive beside the Kithurst Hill car park. Leave the route of the SDW here, walk through the car park, cross the head of the narrow road which feeds it, and take a narrow bridleway along the right-hand side

The pond in Parham Park

Large arable fields spread across the Downs south of Storrington

of a fenced flower meadow. The way soon goes between bushes and then comes to a four-way crossing. Turn left and in a few paces you'll gain a view down to Parham House. The bridleway descends the wooded slope of **Kithurst Hill** and forks halfway. Since the two routes rejoin lower down, take whichever suits.

Emerging from the trees at the foot of the slope the main track curves right, but we go ahead towards a house (Coldharbour). Now swing left into the edge of a field. A few paces later cross back to the right over a stile and walk down the left-hand edge of a meadow. At the bottom left-hand corner cross a footbridge over a minor stream and continue ahead beside a fence. Over another footbridge keep ahead when the path forks, and eventually arrive at a residential area on the southwestern edge of **Storrington**. Ignore the footpath cutting left, and continue ahead on a drive passing a few houses. On coming to Beehive Cottage descend a few steps on the left and follow an enclosed footpath which leads to Amberley Road (the B2139). Turn right to walk into Storrington.

WALK 24

Amberley to The Burgh

Distance	6¾ miles (11km)
Map	OS Explorer 121 Arundel & Pulborough 1:25,000
Start	Amberley Station (TQ 026 118)
Access	By train: Amberley is on the London Victoria to Arundel line.
	By road: via B2139, east of the A29/A284 junction north of
	Arundel.
Parking	At Amberley Station
Refreshments	Pubs, tearooms, restaurants and shop in or near Amberley

Snug at the foot of the South Downs in the Arun valley, Amberley is without question one of the prettiest villages in Sussex, so this walk makes a point of wandering through it before climbing onto the Downs. The route then heads roughly southward into a hidden, almost secretive hollow in the midst of steeply-folding hills, then climbs out by way of a glorious wild flower meadow. It's a richly varied walk which contrasts the banks of the low-lying River Arun with the high crests of the Downs.

From Amberley Station walk down the approach road to the B2139 and turn left. Passing beneath the railway bridge note that refreshments may be obtained at a nearby pub, café and brasserie. Cross the road bridge over the River Arun, and immediately turn right onto a raised footpath alongside the river. On coming to a grey steel footbridge cross to the north bank, turn left and continue upstream along another raised embankment. After about ¾ mile (1.2km) draw level with Bury church, seen across the river, leave the embankment path and turn right (there's a marker post) to walk across a former marshland towards a gate. This marks a crossing of a drainage channel.

Once a much more powerful river, until 1955 a ferry would carry passengers across the **Arun** here, and

135

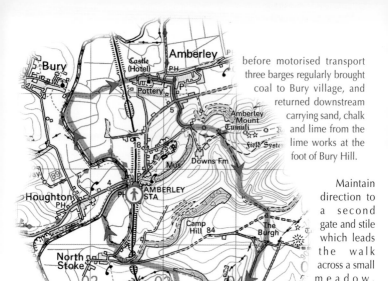

before motorised transport three barges regularly brought coal to Bury village, and returned downstream carrying sand, chalk and lime from the lime works at the foot of Bury Hill.

Maintain direction to a second gate and stile which leads the walk across a small meadow. Beyond a third gate and stile walk ahead to a railway line. Cross the line (caution!) and continue on a footpath which takes you alongside the curtain wall of Amberley Castle (TQ 027 132) and into **Amberley** village.

Amberley lies near the head of what in the Middle Ages was a navigable stretch of the Arun, which answers the need for its castle to protect the village from attack. Built in the second half of the 14th century by the Bishop of Chichester, it was never put to the test, and is now used as a hotel. The church next door is older than the castle, dating from about 1100: it has an elaborately carved archway over the chancel and a faded wall painting thought to be about 800 years old. Amberley has a pub (The Black Horse), a village stores and a number of charming houses and cottages set among old-fashioned country gardens whose flowers cascade over the walls and along the roadside verges.

After passing the church and several attractive houses come to a T-junction in the middle of the village. ▶ Turn right, soon to pass tearoooms as you walk south to the B2139. Cross to the narrow Mill Lane and walk uphill to a junction. Bear left. When the lane curves sharply to the right, leave it for a path (the South Downs Way) rising uphill among trees, then through a bridle gate continue between fences until you reach a broad track. Keep ahead, then branch right when the track forks after a few paces. **Downs Farm** can be seen to the right across a narrow dry valley which sweeps downhill to the south.

Turn left here for the shop.

A short distance along the track it forks once more. Take the right branch again, a grassy alternative to the main track. Making a steady descent it divides again near a gate. Go ahead through the gate and continue down the slope where the way kinks left then right through another gate into a meadowland bowl surrounded by steep hills. The path now angles half-left up the opposite slope – a wonderful wild flower meadow in the early summer. On gaining the head of the slope come to a crossing track at TQ 044 113 – lovely broad views show the mostly arable Downs spreading out in all directions.

Keep ahead across **The Burgh** along the left-hand side of a field, with Arundel Castle on show to the southwest, and at the far end enter a small wood. There's another crossing path, but you continue

Descending from The Burgh, a narrow path takes the path alongside woodland

ahead. Emerging on the far side of the wood, bear right along a bridleway track and, at converging tracks, continue ahead for about ½ mile (800m). Shortly before it curves left, leave the track for a fence-enclosed footpath cutting back and descending to the right. The slope steepens, with the path going down a long flight of steps alongside more woodland. At the foot of the slope come to a crossing bridleway at TQ 038 103, and turn left.

With the wooded slope to your left and a field to your right, walk along the bridleway until you come to a gate and a stile on the right. Over the stile follow the field edge beside a reed-choked drainage channel, then cross a footbridge at the far side and turn right. Crossing two more footbridges, the path is raised between reedy drainage channels. It becomes an enclosed section of trees, bushes and reeds, eventually coming to a stile and an open grass strip with a crossing bridleway. Bear left along the bridleway, soon rising across a sloping meadow to a gate leading onto a track. Continue slightly left ahead along the track which forks soon after. Take the right branch and within a few paces where it turns sharply to the right, keep ahead through a gap in a hedge and among trees as far as a narrow lane on the outskirts of **North Stoke**.

Wander down the slope and, a few paces after passing a house on the right, take a footpath on the left which leads through more bushes and trees, with honeysuckle and dog roses adding colour and fragrance. This leads to a raised path by the River Arun where you turn right and follow the river to the B2139. Turn right, go beneath the railway bridge, then up the approach road to Amberley Station.

Houghton Bridge spans the River Arun at the end of the walk

WALK 25
Burpham to Angmering Park

Distance	6 miles (9.5km)
Map	OS Explorer 121 Arundel & Pulborough 1:25,000
Start	Burpham (TQ 039 089)
Access	By road: Burpham is the northernmost village on a minor No Through Road north of A27 east of Arundel Station. Nearest railway station: Arundel (2 miles)
Parking	Car park behind Burpham Recreation Ground, near The George & Dragon pub (TQ 039 089)
Refreshments	Pub in Burpham

Two attractive villages, a long ramp of downland with expanding views, and a stroll through the woods of Angmering Park are the essential features of this circular outing. Tucked away at the end of a dead-end road on the east bank of the River Arun not far from Arundel, Burpham, and neighbouring Wepham, are small, self-contained communities linked by footpath or narrow lane with easy access to the Downs which rise close by.

The George & Dragon stands in the centre of Burpham, between the church and recreation ground. With your back to the recreation ground walk past the pub, turn right and follow the road leading out of the village, passing Burpham Country House Hotel along the way. On the edge of the village the road makes a sharp turn to the right, and a few paces later you break left into the narrow Coombe Lane. When this ends at a pumping station next to a house, continue ahead on a track. After crossing a stile next to a field gate the way leads into a lovely slope of cropped downland pitted with rabbit burrows.

The way forks at TQ 053 096. Fork right and angle up and across the hillside leading to **Wepham Down**, with views growing in extent as you progress towards

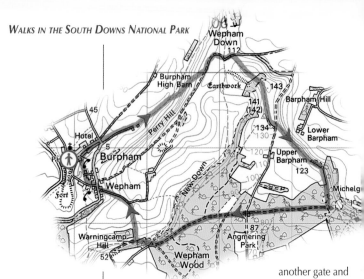

From here Arundel Castle may be seen to the southwest.

another gate and stile near the head of the slope. ◄ Burpham lies below among trees: across the Arun valley woodland clothes the east-facing slope of the Downs; Burpham High Barn is a short way off in the northwest; and beyond that large open fields give the Downs a patchwork appearance.

Above the Arun's valley a path angles across the slope of Wepham Down

Over the stile enter a conservation area, noted for ground-nesting birds, then come to a broad crossing track on the crest of the Downs. Turn left. The track makes a steady curve to the right and is joined by another. In a few paces turn left at a four-way crossing, now heading northeast on a farm track, but after 100 yards go through a bridle gate on the right and walk up the centre of a sloping meadow. At the top of this go through a gap between trees and maintain direction across open downland towards a trig point on **Barpham Hill**. ▶ Shortly before reaching the trig point wander through a gap in an ancient earthwork embankment, marked as a Cross Dyke on the map.

The coast can be seen far off from the exquisite vantage point of this high trail.

Pass to the left of the trig point to join a track leading to a gate. Through this turn left at a major crossing track, and almost immediately swing right to go through a bridle gate and walk ahead, at first among trees and bushes. Cutting across a steep slope you gain a lovely birds-eye view onto the isolated, but attractive buildings of Lower Barpham, beyond which the Downs roll into the far distance. Going through a field gate the bridleway curves to the right and continues alongside a line of beech trees, then on a woodland track which can be muddy at times.

Join a broader track in a clearing, re-enter woodland, and shortly after come to a major crossing track which carries the route of The Monarch's Way. Turn right and remain on this track through woods (carpeted with bluebells in springtime) for about ½ mile (800m) where you then come to an opening with a house on the left at TQ 064 082.

The way continues through the woods as a surfaced track, and a little over ½ mile from the house you come to a multi-junction of bridleways. Walk ahead for a few paces, then take a bridleway descending on the right. After a few paces cross another track and descend on a narrow bridleway among trees. At the foot of the slope join another track and continue ahead for a few more paces. The Monarch's Way now turns left, but we branch right and follow a track which goes along the right-hand edge of a small woodland (The Knell), then continues

Attractive thatched cottage in Wepham

rising through a long woodland shaw at the top of which you come onto a lane, or farm drive, and turn left.

Wandering down the lane, Arundel Castle can be seen once again in the distance. A beautiful thatched cottage stands beside the lane where it comes to a T-junction in **Wepham**. Turn right and a few paces later branch left down a side road. Passing Wepham Farm on the right, and several houses on the left, come to the foot of the slope where you will find a footpath cutting sharply back on the right, with a flight of stone steps leading up to a stile. Over this a fenced footpath carries the way forward. Over a second stile bear left and walk along the edge of a meadow to a third stile. A long flight of steps now takes the path down to a low-lying meadow where a footbridge crosses a stream. In the far corner cross a final stile onto a narrow lane which rises into **Burpham**. Turn left at a T-junction and shortly after reach The George & Dragon in the heart of the village.

WALK 26

Arundel to South Stoke and Burpham

Distance	8 miles (12.5km)
Map	OS Explorer 121 Arundel & Pulborough 1:25,000
Start	Arundel High Street/Mill Road junction (TQ 019 070)
Access	By train: on the Horsham–Arundel–Littlehampton line; by road Arundel is 3½ miles north of Littlehampton at junction of A27/A284
Parking	Several car parks in Arundel. There is also a car park in Burpham (TQ 039 089) – an alternative start
Refreshments	Pubs & cafés in Arundel, pub in Burpham

Contrasts abound on this walk. There's a narrow restricting valley, and the wide open Downs; miles of easy riverside walking, and a steep uphill section; there are woodlands and meadows; the tourist-thronged streets of Arundel, its massive castle and Gothic-style cathedral; and the tiny hamlet of South Stoke, whose 11th-century church is a haven of peace worth visiting, as is the dignified beauty of Burpham, a village magically set between river and downland.

The southern end of Arundel High Street meets Mill Road by the bridge which spans the River Arun. Walk along Mill Road, soon passing the gatehouse entrance to the castle. When the road crosses a bridge over a tributary of the Arun, note that a footbridge offers a safer crossing below and to the right of the road. Almost immediately beyond the bridge a signed footpath cuts left into Arundel Park and continues along the wooded left bank of **Swanbourne Lake**.

Note
Arundel Park is closed each year on 24 March. Dogs and cycles are prohibited at all times. A more open alternative footpath takes the right ▶

(north) bank. To find this continue along the road a short distance. With a Wildfowl Reserve on the right, turn left through a gate (refreshments are available here at Swanbourne Lodge). The two lakeside paths reunite at the northwestern end at TQ 014 083.

Arundel Wildfowl Reserve is run by The Wildfowl and Wetland Trust which was founded in 1946. WWT Arundel has 60 acres of lakes, ponds and reedbeds, and more than 1000 ducks, swans and geese. In addition to a Visitor Centre, the Reserve has seven hides, a restaurant and tea room. It is open daily throughout the year except on Christmas Day.

Over a stile walk ahead through a narrow coombe, or valley, which curves to the right. On coming to a marker post indicating a junction of ways, bear right and climb a steep slope dividing two stems of the valley

Beyond Swanbourne Lake the path enters a narrow coombe

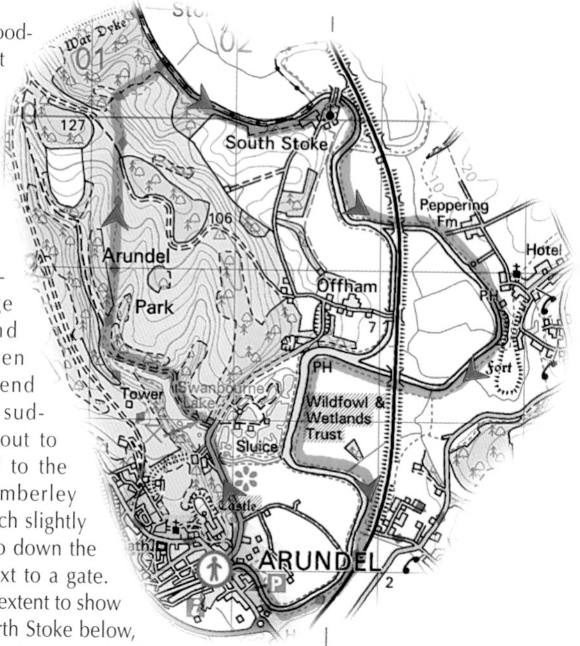

to the right of a wood-
land. Almost at
the head of the
slope cross a
stile and walk
ahead across a
large open grass-
land. Eventually
come to the edge
of a fenced wood-
land (Dry Lodge
Plantation) and
curve left. When
you reach the end
of the wood a sud-
den view opens out to
reveal the Weald to the
north beyond Amberley
Wild Brooks. Branch slightly
right ahead and go down the
slope to a stile next to a gate.
The view grows in extent to show
Houghton and North Stoke below,
the snaking River Arun, Amberley
Mount and the Downs on the far side.

A chalk track now descends along the edge of a
lovely wild flower meadow, and after passing through
some trees you turn right at a crossing path/track.
Shortly after, branch left (there's a signpost) on a more narrow
path descending among trees and bushes, then alongside a flintstone wall which serves as a boundary to
Arundel Park.

Go through a gate in the wall and turn right on a very
pleasant woodland path. Leave the woods by a stile and
walk ahead along the lower edge of a field, at the bottom
corner of which you go through a gateway and along a
bridleway which brings you to some barns at **South Stoke**
Farm. At the end of these turn right beside another flintstone wall and come to a narrow lane. Turn left into the
tiny hamlet of South Stoke and follow the lane past a few

145

houses. It then curves right as a track on the left-hand side of South Stoke churchyard.

> **South Stoke church** dates from the 11th century and is worth a short diversion to visit. Dedicated to St Leonard, it has no electricity so is lit by candles, and in lieu of an organ, a harmonium accompanies hymn singing. The churchyard grass is kept short by grazing sheep. Although simple and bare by comparison with many other downland churches, there is beauty in its simplicity. Enjoy its peace and come away refreshed.

Cross the River Arun by a farm bridge and immediately turn right over a stile onto a raised footpath. At first there are bushes of dog roses between the path and the river which curves around South Stoke, then straightens to the south before curving east again. A side arm of the river then leads the path on a diversion towards Burpham. Cross the railway line and curve to the right below **Peppering Farm**, and wander along a narrow meadow, with the tower of Burpham church seen above some trees. Through a bridle gate the path rises among trees and bushes, then forks. The right branch is the direct route to Arundel, while the recommended left-hand option visits Burpham before rejoing the main path south of the village.

The Burpham path brings you onto a narrow road where you walk ahead, then turn right in front of The George & Dragon pub, which dates from 1736, and come to the village recreation ground. Walk along the left-hand edge, then maintain direction on an enclosed footpath from which the hamlet of Wepham, backed by the Downs, may be seen across a meadow to the left. Descend a flight of steps to rejoin the riverside path, and turn left. Dense reeds largely conceal this minor arm of the Arun until after you've recrossed the railway line, where it then flows into the main river. On the opposite bank can be seen The Black Rabbit pub. The river makes long loops around the edge of water meadows, and brings you close to the railway line again.

Note

Walkers using Arundel Youth Hostel can return to the hostel by crossing the railway line here (caution), and taking the first turning on the left.

Remain on the riverside path into **Arundel**, where it ends. Walk through a yard and out to a street by a bridge. Over this you come to the junction of High Street and Mill Road once more.

ARUNDEL

Arundel is dominated by its castle. Built shortly after the Norman Conquest by Roger Montgomery in order to defend the valley from sea-borne raiders, it was largely destroyed by the Parliamentarians in 1644. Rebuilt in the 18th-century and restored in 1890, it has been in the possession of the Dukes of Norfolk for several centuries. Opposite the castle stands the Catholic cathedral. Despite looking rather like a French Gothic building of the 1300s, it actually dates from the 1870s. The town also has a number of pleasant 18th-century houses and the one-time coaching inn of The Norfolk Arms in the High Street.

Having followed the Arun from South Stoke, the riverside path enters Arundel

WALK 27

Bignor Hill to Sutton

Distance	6¼ miles (10km)
Map	OS Explorer 121 Arundel & Pulborough 1:25,000
Start	Bignor Hill car park (SU 975 130)
Access	By minor road south of Bignor, about 3½ miles northwest of the A29/B2139 junction
Parking	National Trust car park at start of walk
Refreshments	Pub in Sutton

The tiny village of Bignor is known for its Roman villa, and for the fact that Stane Street, the Roman road which led from Chichester to London, passed close by. This walk begins on that Roman road, at a car park where a large oak signpost bears the Roman names for London and Chichester. At first heading northwest along the edge of the Downs, the route then descends its steep and wooded east flank to visit Sutton and Bignor before returning to the downland crest at Westburton Hill. It's another walk of contrasts.

Begin at the southern end of the car park, where a stony track is signed for the South Downs Way heading towards Cocking and Winchester. When the SDW breaks left, keep ahead on the track which aims just to the right of a pair of radio masts. Shortly before entering trees, pause for a moment to enjoy the view behind you, where the distinctive shapes of Chanctonbury Ring and Cissbury Ring can be clearly seen; the heavily wooded Weald spreading to the left, the sea off to the right.

When the track forks within woodland, ignore the left branch and keep ahead. It forks again as you leave the trees, but once again you keep ahead through a gateway and across a gently sloping meadow with more lovely views to enjoy. Pass through another woodland and emerge to yet more fine views as you continue to wander down-hill. Entering trees again the track makes a sharp dog-leg

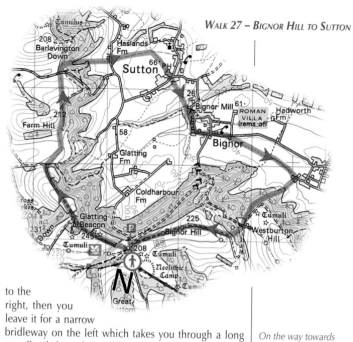

to the
right, then you
leave it for a narrow
bridleway on the left which takes you through a long
woodland shaw, from which occasional views can be
enjoyed to the right.

*On the way towards
Farm Hill the walk
crosses open grassland*

Entering the beech hanger of Farm Wood, follow a track which rises through it, then cuts across the east flank of **Farm Hill** before coming to a large open field with, yet again, a vast panoramic view that demands your attention. At the bottom of the field cross a track and a few paces later come to a junction of paths and bridleways. Take the footpath which cuts back to the right into Northcomb Wood, and follow this as it makes a gentle descent to a broad crossing path.

Note
The original upper section of this path as marked on the OS Explorer map no longer exists, having been destroyed by fallen trees. The route described is the one to follow.

Turn left, and after about 100 yards turn right at a signed junction. The gradient increases as you descend among yew and beech trees and come to the bottom northeast corner of the woods. Over a stile bear half right then walk through the middle of a field to pass along the right-hand side of the ruined Northcomb Barn to reach Folly Lane at SU 971 154.

Across the lane take a bridleway cutting through a large open field towards the village of **Sutton**. On coming to a field boundary on the left, turn right on a crossing path which now takes you southeast to a gate leading into a garden. Walk between an avenue of trees, then alongside a wall, through another gate and between a wall and a fence to reach The White Horse pub at a junction of lanes (SU 979 152).

Turn right then left onto an enclosed footpath signed to Bignor. Cross an open field, go over a stile and walk down a sloping meadow to a pond below **Bignor Mill**. The way skirts round the pond, crosses a footbridge, continues through woodland and across a second footbridge. Out of the woods pass below a house and, through a gate, come onto a lane. Turn right. Passing a row of cottages, follow the lane as its curves left and brings you to Jay's Farm at the entrance to the road which climbs to Bignor Hill car park. Keep ahead to a junction of roads and continue towards West Burton.

About 200 yards along the road, and before reaching a house, go through a gap on the right into a field. During research there was neither signpost nor marked footpath through the crops, but the map shows a right of way angling across this field. As there is a large headland, it may be better to walk around the field boundary to the far southeastern corner (SU 992 142) where a signpost directs the way over a footbridge among trees and bushes, then left into another large field.

Keep along the left-hand edge of this field for about two-thirds of its length, then veer left among some old apple trees and a tiny grassland surrounded by trees. ▶ Among trees the path leads along the right bank of a stream, then crosses a footbridge to the left bank before emerging onto a narrow lane beside a half-timbered house on the edge of **West Burton**. Turn right between houses onto a track. When it forks, with one track curving right into a field, keep ahead to climb the wooded slope of **Westburton Hill**.

Leave the woods at a crossing track near a barn. Walk ahead to a second crossing track and bear right on the South Downs Way. Rising steadily the way leads up to **Bignor Hill**.

Here you pass a mounting block known as **Toby's Stone** (SU 983 133), a replacement memorial to a huntsman who died in 1955, with the lines 'Here he lies where he longed to be/home is the sailor, home from the sea/and the hunter home from the hill.'

Continue over the crown of the hill, which has one of the finest panoramas in this part of the South Downs, and wander down to the car park at the head of the mile-long road from Bignor.

This area is known as a 'pill pond', which was awarded the status of a Common.

WALK 28

Bignor Hill to Slindon

Distance	7¾ miles (12.5km)
Map	OS Explorer 121 Arundel & Pulborough 1:25,000
Start	Bignor Hill car park (SU 975 130) – or Park Lane car park, Slindon (SU 961 077)
Access	By minor road south of Bignor, about 3½ miles northwest of Arundel. For Slindon, take the minor road northeast of the A27/A29 junction 3½ miles west of Arundel.
Parking	National Trust car park at Bignor Hill, or south of Slindon in Park Lane (see above)
Refreshments	Pub in Slindon

Between Bignor Hill and Slindon the Downs offer a mixture of grazing land, arable fields and woodland. It's a peaceful tract of countryside, most of which forms part of the extensive Slindon Estate, and wandering through it there's a distinct possibility of catching sight of fallow deer. The Roman Stane Street is followed at the start, before breaking away to pass alongside Gumber Farm, on which the National Trust has a bothy and small camping area. Beyond the farm the walk is then led along a flint track on the way to Slindon. Slindon itself has some attractive features and makes a viable alternative start to the walk – for this, see alternative start below.

From the southern end of the Bignor Hill car park walk along the stony track of the South Downs Way in the direction of Cocking and Winchester. When it forks near a fenced meadow, branch left, but on coming to a four-way junction leave the SDW and cross directly ahead on a bridleway signed to Gumber Bothy. This raised section is part of the old **Roman road** which led from Chichester to London, and for a while has been adopted by the Monarch's Way.

ROMAN ROAD

The Roman road was built in AD70 for both military and economic purposes to link their regional capital, Chichester (*Noviomagus*), with London (*Londinium*). It was a remarkable piece of engineering, for this road, to which the Saxons later gave the name Stane Street, was 56 miles (90km) long, and was made in three straight lines, one of which went through the 2000 acre estate attached to the Roman villa at Bignor. It first had to cross the Downs, then traverse the sticky clay of the Weald before climbing over the Greensand Hills near Dorking, and the North Downs via the Mole valley and Mickleham Downs. The road was metalled, it had a camber, and was as much as 20–25ft (6–7.5m) wide.

The way leads to a stile which you cross into a sweeping downland meadow with the coast seen several miles ahead, and continue along the raised path as far as the southwestern end of the meadow. Go through a gate on the left and walk towards the buildings of **Gumber Farm** (SU 962 118). On one of these buildings a plaque commemorates the Sussex poet and writer Hilaire Belloc, who had a particular fondness for these Downs.

One of the most popular of Sussex poets is remembered at Gumber Farm

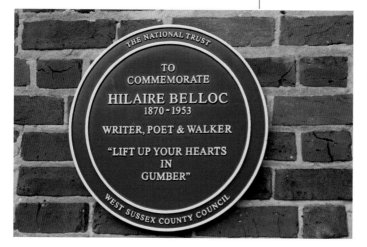

THE NATIONAL TRUST

TO
COMMEMORATE

HILAIRE BELLOC
1870 - 1953

WRITER, POET & WALKER

"LIFT UP YOUR HEARTS
IN
GUMBER"

WEST SUSSEX COUNTY COUNCIL

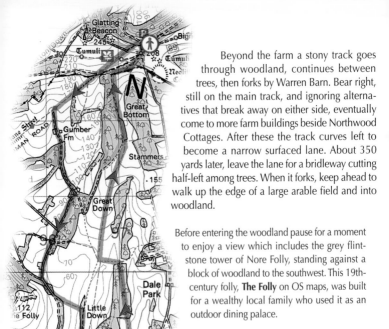

Beyond the farm a stony track goes through woodland, continues between trees, then forks by Warren Barn. Bear right, still on the main track, and ignoring alternatives that break away on either side, eventually come to more farm buildings beside Northwood Cottages. After these the track curves left to become a narrow surfaced lane. About 350 yards later, leave the lane for a bridleway cutting half-left among trees. When it forks, keep ahead to walk up the edge of a large arable field and into woodland.

Before entering the woodland pause for a moment to enjoy a view which includes the grey flint-stone tower of Nore Folly, standing against a block of woodland to the southwest. This 19th-century folly, **The Folly** on OS maps, was built for a wealthy local family who used it as an outdoor dining palace.

When the way forks, curve right and wander through the trees with an open field to the left. The bridleway forks twice, and on both occasions you take the right branch which takes you past Downe's Barn (a clearer view of the folly may be had from here). After this the way becomes a dirt track known as Butt Lane, leading to a narrow road opposite the entrance to Slindon College (SU 960 086). Turn left into Slindon village. After passing the Catholic church a side road, Church Hill, slopes down to the right. This road leads to the 11th-century parish church and an attractive pond. The main walk passes above Church Hill, but soon turns left along Mill Lane at SU 965 084.

Founded by the West Saxons, **Slindon** is located on a tilting shelf of land (the name means 'sloping hill') where the Downs meet the coastal plain leading to the Channel.

154

Alternative start in Slindon

From the car park in Park Lane south of the village, walk up the road to a T-junction and turn left into Slindon. Rising beside houses cross the entrance to Church Hill and keep ahead until Mill Lane breaks to the right. Turn into this lane and join the route as described.

Above Slindon, Mill Lane curves sharply to the right. A big view south may be had over the right-hand hedgerow. On coming to the edge of a wood, turn left on a footpath which immediately forks. Take the right branch, then keep ahead at a crossing bridleway. The path curves to the right and, joining a second crossing path, turns left and soon reaches the southeast corner of the woods near Chichester Lodge. Turn left and walk along the woodland edge beside a fence, then through a projecting finger of trees. On emerging from these bear left, go through a

The view south from Great Down

155

gateway and wander through a large arable field in a valley, with **Dale Park House** seen at its head.

The path brings you into Dencher Wood, a stately woodland comprising mostly beech and yew. At the far end curve left alongside a fence, then through an area of trees and bushes and along the lower edge of a large arable field. A few paces after passing a small corrugated iron shed, come to crossing tracks and turn right to head north through the centre of the field on a bridleway. At the top of this go through a gate and maintain direction across the lovely meadow of **Great Down**, which has a splendid view back to the south.

Another bridle gate at the far end of the meadow leads the way into more woodland. Keep ahead at all junctions as you wander through, until you come to a T-junction of tracks at what is known as Gumber Corner. Turn right onto the Monarch's Way once more, and enjoy another lovely view to the right with the sea far off. About 200 yards from Gumber Corner there's a bench seat beside the track, with a path cutting left beside it. Along this keep ahead at a crossing path and soon arrive at the Bignor Hill car park.

St Mary's church in Slindon

WALK 29

Duncton to Barlavington and Sutton

Distance	5 miles (8km) or 6 miles (9.5km) with Burton Mill Pond option
Map	OS Explorer 121 Arundel & Pulborough 1:25,000
Start	Dye House Lane, Duncton (SU 960 171) or Burton Mill Pond car park (SU 978 180)
Access	By bus from Petworth or Chichester; Duncton is on A285, 3 miles south of Petworth. Burton Mill Pond car park is on a minor road east of the A285, 1 mile north of Duncton
Parking	Burton Mill Pond Nature Reserve car park
Refreshments	Pubs in Duncton and Sutton

There are two options to begin this walk. For those arriving by bus, the main walk starts in the village of Duncton; the alternative is for walkers with their own transport – in which case their route is a mile longer than the main option, for it begins at a car park at the northern end of Burton Mill Pond, northeast of Duncton. It remains below the Downs, in the lush countryside of the Western Weald with its rich diversity of parkland, fields, woods and meadows, two adjoining lakes, three villages and a water mill. But the wooded slopes of the Downs form a backdrop, an ever-looming presence whose enticement is not difficult to resist on this occasion, thanks to the constantly changing nature of the route.

Starting at Duncton, about 100 yards north of The Cricketers pub, the narrow Dye House Lane breaks away from the A285 heading east, soon flanked by woodland. After passing a large house the lane narrows, curves to the right and slopes into a dip. Before long it becomes a stony track leading to a few buildings and a lovely pond at **Duncton Mill** – a delightful scene. As the way rises beyond the mill pond, take a bridleway on the left, climbing among trees on the edge of Fountain Copse.

Out of Duncton the walk enjoys this tranquil scene near Duncton Mill

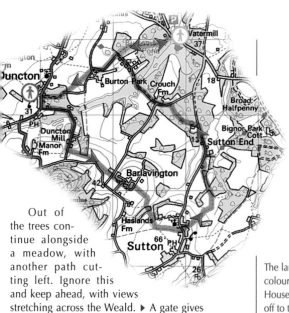

Out of the trees continue alongside a meadow, with another path cutting left. Ignore this and keep ahead, with views stretching across the Weald. ▶ A gate gives access onto a narrow lane where you immediately turn

The large cream-coloured Burton House can be seen off to the left.

Burton Mill Pond start

From the entrance to the car park head west for a few paces (towards the A285), then go through a gate on the left and walk ahead into woodland, which forms part of the Burton and Chingford Ponds Local Nature Reserve. After a while the path briefly leaves the woods before entering the more open woodland of Black Pond Copse, then comes onto a drive leading through **Burton Park**. Keep ahead towards Burton House where the drive curves to the right, then left by a tiny Norman church. Shortly after passing the church leave the drive for a grass path cutting half-right ahead guided by fences. This leads to East Wood and rejoins the drive. Turn right and follow this to the A285 on the edge of Duncton at SU 961 173. Bear left, and about 180 yards later come to Dye House Lane to join the main walk (see p.157).

The tiny hamlet of Barlavington is tucked against the foot of the Downs

left, cross a stile and take a path aiming half-right across a meadow, then beside a garden boundary to the bottom corner where a stile takes you down a slope onto a narrow lane. Cross directly ahead. Over a footbridge the continuing path rises through a tunnel of trees, passes below a massive yew then comes onto a stony drive leading to another narrow lane in the tiny hamlet of **Barlavington**. Bear left, then enter the grounds of the lovely little Norman church of St Mary (SU 972 161).

Leave the churchyard at its southeast corner and go ahead on a farm drive, soon curving towards some timber-walled barns – before reaching the largest of these, look to the left where the old church can be seen behind a crooked-roofed barn, creating a scene straight out of a Thomas Hardy novel.

Opposite the large barns turn right on a track. At first there's a view to the right where Barlavington Down rises abruptly then, entering a meadow, you walk ahead down its right-hand edge. About two thirds of the way down the slope cross a tall ladder-stile on the right, then continue down to a wooded corner where a clear stream has to be crossed before you go steeply up through woods. Out of the trees maintain direction along the edge of a scrubby meadow, to reach a crossing path in an open field. Turn left along the path which soon takes you beside tennis courts where two bench seats tempt you to rest, with a view across the field to the Downs. The way then goes down a slope to a road in Sutton.

> **Note**
> Should you be in need of refreshment, The White Horse pub is located about 250 yards along the road to the right.

Bear left, and a few paces before reaching the church, turn right into the very narrow School Lane. When it bends to the right keep ahead on a grass path and cross a stile, after which the way is squeezed by trees and bushes before being released into a sloping meadow. Walk down the right-hand side, then through a strip of trees and out to a second meadow. Here you cut ahead to the opposite side, then bear right along the tree-lined boundary. Coming to the lower section of the meadow (rich in wild flowers), turn left and at the bottom left-hand corner you will find a stile. Over this bear right alongside Winters Copse.

In the next corner a footbridge gives access to yet another meadow where you walk directly ahead to a second footbridge by some gorse bushes. A few paces over this come to a third footbridge, after which the path takes you along the right-hand side of a thatched cottage and onto a narrow road at SU 983 164.

Turn right, and about 600 yards later, after passing Old Poor House, turn left on a drive heading through woodland to Sutton End House. When the drive curves left to pass through the gates of the house, go ahead on a bridleway through mixed woods. This brings you to another narrow lane where you bear left. When it makes a sharp bend near **Crouch Farm** walk ahead through a gateway and continue on what becomes

The outflow from this lake pours into Burton Mill Pond, which remains hidden among trees on the right.

a sunken path, then an embankment overlooking Chingford Pond. ◄

Through a gate the way continues and soon comes onto a drive beside what appears to be a village green, but is a private residential area within Burton Park.

Return to Burton Mill Pond

When the drive makes a sharp left-hand bend at SU 971 178, walkers who left their vehicle at the Burton Mill Pond car park should turn right, go through a gate and retrace the initial part of the walk through woods as far as the country road a few paces from the car park.

Near the car park **Burton Mill** stands on the site of a 17th-century iron forge, the mill pond having been a hammer pond providing a head of water to work the forge. Pig iron would have been brought here for reheating and hammering to reduce its carbon content before being turned into tools or weapons. In 1635 a visitor described the 'hot swarthy Vulcans, sweating, puffing, hammering, drawing out those rusty sows [pig iron] into barrs.'

Those who began the walk in Duncton should bear left along the drive, then curve right with it near Burton House. Shortly after the drive turns left by the little church, take the grass path cutting half-right ahead. When this brings you to East Wood and the continuing drive, turn right and walk into Duncton.

As a child, **Hilaire Belloc** became a friend of the Wright-Biddulphs who owned Burton House, and in a chalet in the grounds he later wrote *The Four Men*.

WALK 30

Singleton to Littlewood Farm

Distance	5½ miles (8.8km)
Map	OS Explorer 120 Chichester, South Harting & Selsey 1:25,000
Start	Singleton (SU 876 131)
Access	By bus from Midhurst or Chichester. Singleton is 6 miles north of Chichester on the A286
Parking	With discretion in the village
Refreshments	Pub and café in Singleton, pub in Charlton

Standing mostly on the east side of the main Chichester road, where it turns north to Midhurst, the old heart of Singleton is grouped around a duckpond with lovely thatched or flint-walled cottages. Nearby stands the pub, with the Saxon church just to the south. The intermittent Lavant stream flows from the east, and the Downs rise on every side. This walk makes a circuit of the neighbouring hills and woodlands before returning through water meadows in the Lavant's valley.

At the southwestern end of Singleton a drive breaks north of the A286 between the last house and the village

The attractive heart of Singleton, a few paces from the A286

playing field. Walk along this drive, enter the playing field and pass behind the cricket pavilion where a stile leads into a meadow. After a few paces cross a second stile on the right, and another on the left which takes a footpath into the National Trust-owned Drovers Estate. This very pleasant path rises gently through a tunnel of trees and across a bridge over the cutting of a dismantled railway. A few paces beyond this bridge climb a few concrete steps, then over another stile into a steeply sloping meadow rich in wild flowers (SU 871 134).

The way rises onto **Hat Hill**, from whose slope views encompass the Lavant's valley and its walling Downs. ◄ At the top of the meadow enter a hilltop field and continue along its left-hand edge. Go through a gate, maintain direction to the top left-hand corner, where you cross a stile on the left, then take a continuing path alongside the woodland known as Puttock's Copse.

On reaching a crossing track, turn right and wander downhill, ignoring an alternative track branching right into the woods. Down the slope stands Downley Cottage, a truly remote but attractive dwelling standing

The only jarring intrusion is the march of pylons carrying high-voltage power cables.

alone with a fine view north across a swathe of arable farmland backed by more woods. The track curves in front of the cottage, then cuts sharply to the left to score along the right-hand boundary of the field overlooked by Downley Cottage. Banks of bracken, a few trees and scrambling bushes of dog roses mark the edge of the field until you reach the mature woodland of **Wellhanger Copse**.

The track curves round the end of the woodland and passes beside the flint-and-timber built Middle Barn. Keep alongside Wellhanger Copse until the track swings left then right towards farm buildings. Just after passing these the track goes between the brick uprights that once supported a bridge over the now-dismantled railway that ran south to Chichester. A few paces on come to **Littlewood Farm** and the A286 at SU 873 150.

Turn left and walk along the grass verge of this busy road for about ¼ mile (400m), then cross with care to a narrow tarmac lane cutting back to the right. A few paces along the lane take a bridleway on the left, rising

After passing Downley Cottage, the walk takes the headland of a large field

through woods. After climbing a short way it brings you onto the lane once more. Bear left, then right a few paces later onto the continuing bridleway which leads through Nightingale Wood, part of **Singleton Forest**. When the bridleway track forks, ignore the right branch and keep ahead. This eventually leads to the edge of the woods and a crossing track. Turn left and, leaving the woods, slope downhill between hedges to reach a four-way junction near the outbuildings of **Broadham House** at SU 888 146.

Walk ahead up a sloping meadow and curve right at the top to reach another multi-junction of tracks. Go through a gateway on the left onto a stony crossing track, where you bear right then left on joining another track. Shortly after it begins to slope downhill, note a gate on the left; but on your right a signpost is partly hidden among trees, indicating a narrow footpath. This takes you up among trees, then over a stile into a meadow, with **Levin Down** rising ahead. Wander along the left-hand side of this meadow until you come to a bridle gate giving access to woodland. Through the gate the path leads across a steep slope among trees, then enters Levin Down Nature Reserve by way of a stile.

The name **Levin Down** is thought to come from Leaven Doune, meaning Leave Alone, referring to the area being free from crops.

The path now goes through a long region of scrub with views east to Court Hill, south to Charlton Down with the grandstand of Goodwood Racecourse seen on the crown of the hill, and down to the houses of Charlton in the valley ahead. Through a gate above Ware Barn the path continues among bushes, now sloping downhill to another gate and alongside a fence to leave the Nature Reserve. Descend across a sloping meadow to a kissing gate giving onto a narrow road, then turn left into **Charlton**.

Turn right at the crossroads, and just before coming to a house on the left, go through a small gate on the right into water meadows on the south side of the River Lavant – an intermittent stream. On the far side of these meadows the path leads to a residential area of Singleton where you walk between fences, then cross a street directly ahead into a close. The way now goes right then left alongside houses and brings you to the Saxon church of St Mary. Turn right to a road, then left to pass The Partridge Inn on the way to the A286 where the walk began.

Note

Before leaving Singleton, a visit to the nearby Weald and Downland Open Air Museum (on the road leading to Goodwood Racecourse) is highly recommended. In an area of 35 acres a number of fascinating old buildings (prime examples of vernacular architecture) have been rescued from demolition and re-erected in their original state.

Flint, thatch and roses – a quintessential downland cottage in Singleton

WALK 31

West Stoke to Kingley Vale and Stoughton

Distance	6½ miles (10.5km)
Map	OS Explorer 120 Chichester, South Harting & Selsey 1:25,000
Start	West Stoke car park (SU 825 088)
Access	By minor road 2 miles west of A286 at Mid Lavant, north of Chichester
Parking	The car park is located west of West Stoke House
Refreshments	Pub in Stoughton

There are three main features to this walk. The first is the Nature Reserve of Kingley Vale, noted for its wonderful old yew trees that clothe the slopes of Stoke Down. The second is the ridge above Kingley Vale, where a row of four burial mounds appear like the humps of a camel, from which far-reaching views may be had. And the third main feature is the peaceful village of Stoughton, with its Saxon church and welcoming pub. But these are not all, for the route has plenty of other highlights to commend it. Choose a day of settled weather and take your time, for there's much to absorb and enjoy.

From the western end of the car park wander along a well-made stony footpath heading north between fields towards the wooded slope of Stoke Down. It passes through a strip of woodland and eventually meets a crossing bridleway at the entrance to **Kingley Vale** Nature Reserve (SU 825 099). Enter the reserve through a gate near an upright wooden sculpture, and turn left onto a footpath – but note the unmanned information building (a field museum) standing partly secluded among trees near the sculpture; it's well worth a visit before resuming the walk.

Cutting to the left away from the sculpture, the path is flanked by trees, with a bridleway beyond a fence running parallel with it – this bridleway will be taken near the end of the walk. Meanwhile the path within

KINGLEY VALE NATURE RESERVE

Established in 1954 Kingley Vale Nature Reserve is noted for its magnificent yew forest, said to be the largest in Britain. Yew trees flourish on many downland slopes, but those at Kingley Vale are thought to be among the oldest living plants in the country. At the foot of the slope behind the field museum (but not on our route), the finest and strangest of these trees may be found. Some gnarled old specimens create arches, tunnels and caves,

their branches bending to the ground where they take root and reappear as neighbouring trees. The forest fans out and spreads up the slope towards the ridge, allowing only spokes of light through – even on the brightest of days. Designated as a Special Area of Conservation, the reserve is rich in wildlife, including fallow deer, 33 species of breeding butterfly and 57 of breeding birds. Orchids appear in open grassy areas, and from the ridge crest above the forest a broad panoramic view makes the climb to reach it worthwhile. The piece of sculpture at the reserve's southern entrance, *The Spirit of Kingley Vale*, was carved by Walter Bailey from a single piece of yew taken from a tree destroyed by the great storm of October 1987.

the nature reserve turns abruptly to the right and begins to ascend the slope. ▶ As height is gained the path gradually curves to the right, enters the woods and rises through the cool shade of a yew grove before emerging through a kissing gate near the first of the Devil's Humps burial mounds at SU 819 110. A splendid view may be had from these; in one direction Chichester and the sea, in the other the lovely valley of the little River Emms.

The Devil's Humps are Bronze Age burial mounds dating from 2000–800BC. Sadly they were plundered by treasure seekers in the 19th century. Between the third and fourth of these humps The Tansley Stone commemorates

Along the way there are a few markers to indicate that it is part of a nature trail.

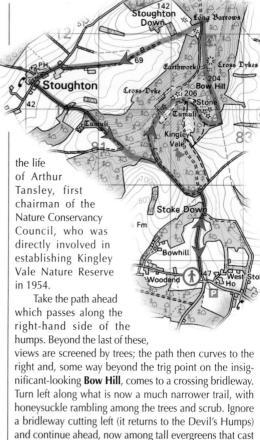

the life of Arthur Tansley, first chairman of the Nature Conservancy Council, who was directly involved in establishing Kingley Vale Nature Reserve in 1954.

Take the path ahead which passes along the right-hand side of the humps. Beyond the last of these, views are screened by trees; the path then curves to the right and, some way beyond the trig point on the insignificant-looking **Bow Hill**, comes to a crossing bridleway. Turn left along what is now a much narrower trail, with honeysuckle rambling among the trees and scrub. Ignore a bridleway cutting left (it returns to the Devil's Humps) and continue ahead, now among tall evergreens that cast permanent shade, until you emerge onto another track by an open meadow on **Stoughton Down**. ◄

There is a view overlooking the Emms valley.

Beyond the meadow turn left on a bridleway that edges another section of woodland, at the end of which a seat tempts you to relax with the Emms valley stretching ahead. From here the bridleway descends for more than a mile without shade; at first between fences, it then joins a farm track leading past large barns before coming

170

The fence-lined path that leads to Stoughton

onto a road beside an attractive house on the outskirts of **Stoughton**. Bear left into the village, passing the Hare and Hound pub, then a road branching right to the Saxon church of St Mary which dates from around 1050. About 100 yards beyond this turning bear left onto a concrete drive by the side of Tythe Barn House (SU 801 114). This soon becomes a track rising once more onto the Downs.

> You pass on the way a **memorial** to a young Polish airman who died in November 1940 when his Hurricane crashed into the field on the left following aerial combat. The headland of the left-hand field is massed with wild flowers in early summer, and beside the memorial simple stone slabs have been placed as seats to encourage rest and contemplation.

The track continues, with the gradient becoming steeper as you pass through a brief belt of woodland, then winds up to a more dense woodland cover. On the edge of this upper woodland another stone slab has been placed at a serene viewpoint.

Dog roses brighten hedgerows in spring and summer

Through beechwoods the track climbs onto the crest of the Downs where an open meadow stretches to the right. Ignoring alternative paths and bridleways keep ahead, soon sloping downhill through more woods of beech and yew, then opening to big views to Chichester Cathedral ahead, and off to the right to Hayling and Thorney Islands and the sea beyond. The bridleway eventually brings you to the entrance to Kingley Vale Nature Reserve where you then turn right to return to the car park.

WALK 32

Compton to East Marden

Distance	5 miles (8km)
Map	OS Explorer 120 Chichester, South Harting & Selsey 1:25,000
Start	The Coach and Horses, Compton (SU 776 148)
Access	By bus from Petersfield and Chichester. Compton is on the B2146 about 4 miles south of South Harting
Parking	With discretion in the village
Refreshments	Pub, shop and café in Compton

An attractive village at the start, and two small hamlets on the walk, add to the interest of this circuit which takes place entirely within the Downs. Since there are neither escarpments nor hilltops to grant extensive views, pleasures will be found in other scenes – lovely small woods and woodland shaws, intimate little valleys, ancient churches and well-heads, and the ease with which one path or trackway links with another. It's a mostly undemanding walk, but it does have some steep uphill and downhill sections.

With the Coach and Horses pub on one side of the village square, and the shop and tearoom on the other, walk along the left-hand side of the well-head feature in the centre of the square and branch left along a side street. Within a few paces follow a track on the left at the end of a flintstone wall, and passing Sawmill Barn enter a meadow. Walk ahead along its right-hand edge, and on reaching the meadow corner go through a gateway, bear left, and cross a stile into a field. Bear half-right and wander across this field to the woodland of Gold Mine Plantation. Entering the wood turn left on a bridleway track.

Emerging from the woods the way goes along the left-hand edge of a field, and on reaching a minor road, note the mound on the right. This is the site of an ancient long barrow known as **Bevis's Thumb**. Cross the road directly ahead

Off to the left you may be able to see the large National Trust owned house, Uppark, jutting above the trees.

onto a continuing bridleway track that has been adopted as part of the Western Downs Cycle Route. Keep along the right-hand side of a large field in a pleasant landscape of arable fields and woodland. ◀

Near the end of the first field section at SU 790 158, cross a stile on the right to follow a footpath alongside the woods of **Fernbeds Down**. A gap in a hedge carries the route forward when the woods end, with a second stile giving access to a path on the left-hand side of a meadow, at the far corner of which you turn left and enter another meadow by way of yet more stiles. Walk ahead towards more woods, but a few paces before coming to a telegraph pole, a signpost directs the path half-right across the meadow to its top right-hand corner, where a multi-junction of paths will be found by some pine trees. Turn right and walk south, initially alongside more pine trees. At the far end of the meadow, a few paces to the right of the corner, come onto a country road at a T-junction (SU 796 155).

Take the road directly ahead (direction Up Marden) for about 20 paces, then cross a stile on the left where a narrow footpath goes down the edge of a grove of beech trees, then over another stile angle half-right down a sloping meadow and continue through the adjoining field. Through a gap in a strip of trees, maintain direction across the next field. At the far corner go through

A thatched well-head stands at the heart of East Marden

some more trees and onto a track which leads to a lane at SU 804 148.

Keep ahead and you will shortly enter **East Marden**, with a few houses on the left. As you approach a road junction note a stile on the right, which takes the walk on to Up Marden. But before crossing this, it would be worth continuing a few paces to the hub of this tiny village where the old but simple church stands to the left, and in the middle of a triangle of roads there's a thatched well-head with the old winching mechanism beneath it, a charming discovery.

To resume the walk cross the stile a few paces northwest of the well-head and follow a footpath slightly right ahead through a meadow, then veer left to another stile in a fence. Over this bear left along the edge of a large field following a line of telegraph poles. At the bottom of the field curve right, then coming to a telegraph pole cross a stile on the left, descend a few steps, and walk ahead to Battines Hill Wood.

The path now climbs steeply through the wood, keeps ahead at a crossing path and emerges from the

175

trees to maintain direction along the boundary of a field. At the far end come to a road on the outskirts of **Up Marden**, a hamlet even smaller than East Marden. Turn left, and after passing Up Marden Farm, turn right along a stony track which very soon passes to the right of the semi-hidden 13th-century church of St Michael.

> **St Michael's church** is a gem of ancient simplicity. More than 700 years old, it has no electricity so is lit by candles. Faded wall paintings adorn two of the walls. Spend a few minutes inside and think of the countless generations of South Downs dwellers who have been baptised, married and buried here – and consider how the landscape outside may have changed since the foundations of this place of worship were first dug.

The track continues beyond the church between hedges and trees that screen fields on either side. When the track ends, continue ahead on a bridleway sloping downhill between more trees to become almost a sunken track. This gives out at a confluence of fields where you maintain direction on a grassy bridleway bordered by more trees and bushes, then through a brief woodland strip and along the right-hand edge of a field before walking alongside a small plantation of pine trees.

Come to a track and bear left, then almost immediately turn right onto a footpath cutting down the boundary of a sloping field, with the houses of Compton now appearing in the valley below. The gradient steepens, and at the foot of the slope you cross a stile beside a field gate to find a multi-junction of bridleways and footpaths. Take the lower bridleway to the right which leads onto a stony track, and this brings you into Compton by the village primary school. Just beyond this you arrive back by the Coach and Horses pub.

WALK 33

Harting Down to Beacon Hill and Telegraph House

Distance	5 miles (8km)
Map	OS Explorer 120 Chichester, South Harting & Selsey 1:25,000
Start	Harting Down car park above South Harting (SU 790 181)
Access	Via B2141 about 1 mile southeast of South Harting
Parking	National Trust pay and display car park on Harting Down
Refreshments	None on route

Above South Harting the grassland of Harting Down draws visitors to walk, fly their kites, exercise their dogs, enjoy a picnic or simply to gaze at the incomparable view. The South Downs Way creeps along the northern rim of this meadow, and by following that route eastwards the panorama expands so that all of West Sussex (it seems) is revealed. This walk diverts from the SDW to cross the high point of Beacon Hill, then rejoins it to climb over Pen Hill before heading south into a more secretive fold of the Downs. It then returns northward through an avenue of copper beech trees before striking away once more to explore Little Round Down on a devious return to the car park on Harting Down. It's a splendid walk with pleasures all the way.

South Harting can be seen from the start of the walk

177

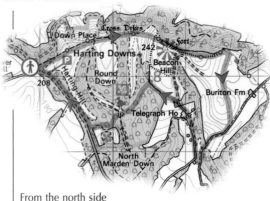

The view over the Weald is simply magnificent and growing in extent as you progress.

From the north side of the National Trust car park walk across the meadow to the crossing path of the South Downs Way from where you have a direct view of South Harting, dominated by the green copper broach spire of its church. Turn right and wander eastwards. ◀ After crossing Harting Down the SDW becomes a broad chalk track sloping downhill between bushes and trees to enter the 'dry valley' of Bramshott Bottom at the foot of **Beacon Hill**. The SDW turns right here, but we go straight up the steep west flank of Beacon Hill and through a gate onto its crown. A few paces to the right of the path a trig point rewards with another splendid panoramic view. ◀

Beacon Hill is the site of a 40-acre Iron Age hillfort.

Continue over the hilltop and descend the very steep eastern side where you rejoin the track of the South Downs Way to climb Pen Hill, from whose summit yet another panoramic view will encourage you to pause in an attempt to absorb the rich tapestry of the landscape laid out below. Over Pen Hill the track descends to woodland, but when the SDW goes into the trees, we take a path along the right-hand edge. On coming to a crossing track (a 'restricted byway') turn right and follow it as it scores a way between arable fields. At the end of the field section continue ahead, soon walking among bushes and trees. When these finish, open fields stretch on either side, and you soon pass above secluded

Buriton Farm – one of many such lonely farms found scattered across the Downs.

The way arrives at a lovely grove of beeches through which you join a track coming from Buriton Farm. Turn half-right and soon come to another junction. Ignore the bridleway branching left, and continue ahead on what appears to be a raised track between fields. Curving, the track rises into the woods of Germanleith Copse, and on coming to a signed junction, turn sharply back to the right through a gateway and wander along a grass track to pass to the right of a bungalow, then on a tarmac drive which takes you along an avenue of copper beech trees on the approach to **Telegraph House**.

> **Telegraph House** is so named because it stands on the site of one of the 19th-century telegraph relay stations created in order to keep the Admiralty in London in touch with the fleet at Portsmouth. When semaphore signals were replaced by the electric telegraph in 1849, the relay station was no longer needed and the house became derelict. It was bought in 1900 by Earl Russell, whose brother, the philospher Bertrand Russell, later turned it into an experimental school with his wife Dora. The school closed in 1934.

When the drive forks just beyond Yew Tree Cottage take the right branch. It curves round to the left, and when it goes through a gateway, continue ahead on a fence-enclosed track, from which Telegraph House can be glimpsed to the left. Passing through a gate the track forks. Take the left branch, in effect straight ahead, once more on the route of the South Downs Way heading for Bramshott Bottom and Harting Down. It's a pleasant section which goes along the left-hand edge of a large field, through a bridle gate and eventually comes to a marker post indicating a path breaking left. Follow this grass path, which is closely cropped by rabbits and flanked by gorse, scrub and trees, descending the slope of Little Round Down. ▶ At the foot of the slope come to a crossing path at SU 801 174. Keep ahead and go through a

From here the roof of Uppark (a large 17th-century house owned by the National Trust, in which the mother of HG Wells was once housekeeper) can be seen above the trees.

Walkers descend the steep slope of Beacon Hill on Harting Down

gate to climb a wooded slope. The path soon curves left by some yew trees. Drawing level with a meadow on the left, come to a junction of paths by a fine beech tree and turn right. Through a kissing gate the continuing path edges the woods alongside a meadow, then veers into the woods. Once again emerge from the trees, cross a stile and walk up the meadow as far as another kissing gate which takes you back into the woods. About 100 yards later turn right on a crossing path which brings you to the meadow on Harting Down near the National Trust car park.

WALK 34

East Meon to Salt Hill

Distance	5 miles (8km)
Map	OS Explorer 119 Meon Valley or 132 Winchester 1:25,000
Start	East Meon church (SU 681 223)
Access	By bus from Winchester via West Meon, and from Petersfield and Bishops Waltham. East Meon is on a minor road 3 miles east of West Meon
Parking	Workhouse Lane Car Park, by East Meon sports pavilion (SU 677 222)
Refreshments	Pubs and shop in East Meon

The Meon valley offers some of the most rewarding walks of the western Downs, and East Meon, one of its loveliest villages, is almost surrounded by hills that seduce with a promise of great views. This particular itinerary underlines that promise, for there's a whole string of vantage points from which to enjoy truly memorable views, the best of all being found among the high country between Salt Hill and Small Down.

Walk through the churchyard of All Saints' church to its top left-hand corner where a footpath rises among trees and, crossing a stile, takes you into the bottom of a sloping meadow. Walk ahead alongside a fence, then over a second stile to maintain direction across another meadow towards a stile beside a field gate. Over this come onto the drive of a house where you turn left onto a narrow lane. Turn right for a few paces, then cross a stile on the left by two field gates, and bear right along the top edge of a large field sweeping into the Meon valley.

Continue along the edge of the next field with views towards **Drayton**, then enter a large sloping meadow. Directly opposite, in the far boundary hedge, a stile will take the footpath onward, but to reach it the official right-of-way traces the left-hand boundary, although in

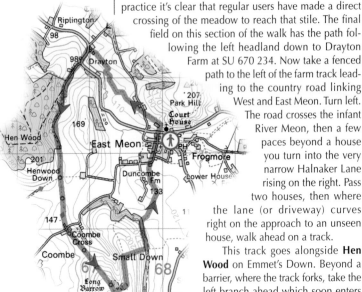

practice it's clear that regular users have made a direct crossing of the meadow to reach that stile. The final field on this section of the walk has the path following the left headland down to Drayton Farm at SU 670 234. Now take a fenced path to the left of the farm track leading to the country road linking West and East Meon. Turn left. The road crosses the infant River Meon, then a few paces beyond a house you turn into the very narrow Halnaker Lane rising on the right. Pass two houses, then where the lane (or driveway) curves right on the approach to an unseen house, walk ahead on a track.

This track goes alongside **Hen Wood** on Emmet's Down. Beyond a barrier, where the track forks, take the left branch ahead which soon enters the beechwood, but keeps close to its left-hand edge. When the woodland track forks again, keep on the left branch – the two stems actually run parallel for some time. After the wood comes to an end, the way continues through a woodland shaw and brings you to a crossing track at SU 666 217.

Keep directly ahead, now on the South Downs Way, through a continuing woodland shaw. When this ends, a brief glimpse may be had across fields to the west where Old Winchester Hill dominates, but then hedges hide the view before you come to a narrow road and a few houses at **Coombe Cross**. Take the track opposite (still the SDW), which narrows to a footpath-sized bridleway after a few paces.

Now heading southeast the way rises between trees, making a steady ascent of **Salt Hill**, from whose summit beautiful and wide-ranging views may be enjoyed. The

Above East Meon, Salt Hill overlooks a vast sweep of country

best views are to be had from a path junction marked by a signpost about 400 yards north of two tall radio towers. Leave the SDW here, cross the stile and wander roughly eastward across a folding downland meadow. Go down the slope and then directly up the opposite slope to a field gate in the left-hand boundary fence. An exquisite panorama is now revealed, with Butser Hill, the highest of the South Downs at 886ft (270m) crowned by a mast to the east, with a far-off sweep of downland ridges fading blue with distance to the left of that. ▶

The valley below is a patchwork of green, yellow and gold in summer, and across it to the north Park Hill looms above East Meon's church spire.

Through the gate walk across the grass crest of **Small Down**, with those glorious views being rearranged as you progress towards a second field gate. Through this turn right and descend alongside a fence, then cross a stile and continue steeply down the slope, at the foot of which you come onto a track by another field gate. Turn left and walk along the lower edge of the meadow to its far right-hand corner where a gate gives access to a path descending among trees. Over a stile continue along the right headland of a field, with a cottage seen slightly left ahead behind a group of trees. At the corner of the field

At the foot of the Downs a series of field paths lead back to East Meon

go through a gap and follow a path rising through the middle of the next field.

On the far side turn left and wander along the field edge towards Duncoombe Farm, then go through a metal kissing gate and down a sloping meadow to a second kissing gate. A short distance beyond this join a narrow road. Bear right and follow it into the heart of **East Meon**.

> **East Meon** is notable, not only for its many pretty cottages, the flint-walled All Saints church (whose grey broach spire can be seen for miles around), and the 15th-century Court House, but for the River Meon which rises nearby and runs below and alongside the main street with little bridges that span it. Izaak Walton, the 17th-century author of *The Compleat Angler*, stayed here to fish the river for trout, and one of the two village pubs bears his name.

WALK 35

East Meon to Small Down

Distance	6 miles (9.5km)
Map	OS Explorer 119 Meon Valley or 132 Winchester 1:25,000
Start	East Meon church (SU 681 223)
Access	By bus from Winchester via West Meon, and from Petersfield and Bishops Waltham. East Meon is on a minor road 3 miles east of West Meon.
Parking	Workhouse Lane Car Park by East Meon sports pavilion (SU 677 222)
Refreshments	Pubs and shop in East Meon

This second of our walks from East Meon makes a clockwise circuit with high points on both sides of the valley. Whilst never straying far from the village, it explores a variety of landscapes that underscore the great beauty and timeless quality of the upper Meon valley.

From the top left-hand corner of All Saints' churchyard take the footpath which goes alongside a fence among trees, then up a flight of stone steps and over a stile into a steeply sloping meadow. Walk uphill beside a line of trees, and on coming to a fence enclosing a field, bear right to wander across the upper slopes of **Park Hill** directly above the church spire. From here a lovely view south takes your attention beyond the village to where Small Down (which will be crossed at the end of the walk) is backed by the radio masts on Wether Down. ▸

Butser Hill can be seen to the southeast.

The way curves around the hillside and brings you to a stile next to a field gate. Maintain direction towards **Park Farm**, but after about 100 yards angle down the slope to the corner of the meadow where another stile takes the walk ahead. This brings you onto a narrow lane by a pond in front of Park Farm at SU 685 233.

Park Hill provides a direct view onto the rooftops of East Meon

Cross the lane onto a track beside Park Cottage and walk along the left headland of a large field. The track curves right at the end of the field, shortly after which you branch left when it forks. Now walking down the left-hand side of a smaller field, come to a crossing track and turn right. After passing beneath high voltage power cables the track forks again at the end of the field. Branch left, and after a few paces branch right when it forks again, this time cutting sharply back to the right, then twisting downhill through woodland.

Emerging from the woods the tall mast on Butser Hill can be seen directly ahead across the valley. At the foot of the slope the track forks yet again. Take the lower branch, a grass bridleway along the lower edge of a field which leads to a country road beside a cottage. Turn right (direction East Meon), and after passing a bus stop, the road curves to the right. Leave it here and walk ahead on a track (a byway) known as Cumber's Lane which takes you below **Barrow Hill**. After almost ½ mile (800m) come to a multi-junction of tracks. Keep directly ahead (the left-hand of two forward routes) and this will eventually bring you to another very narrow lane at SU 696 214.

Turn right, and after about 30 paces bear left on a narrow path crowded at first with bushes, but then improving as you come to a drive by the handsome and appropriately named Fishpond Cottage. Wander down the drive to Harvesting Lane, then turn right. At a junction of roads bear left, and in a few paces pass Parsonage Barn. On coming to the next junction by Lower Farm, turn left, and immediately after passing some large barns on the right, take a footpath which goes along the right-hand edge of a field.

At the top right-hand corner turn left (a view through a gap on the right shows the spire of East Meon church), and about halfway along the boundary hedge, go through a gap and walk along the right-hand edge of the adjacent field, at the corner of which you come onto a track rising and curving gently to the right. Through a gate immediately turn left to climb the steeply sloping hillside. Keep to the right of some trees, cross a stile in the boundary fence (note a simple stone seat with a view off to the right) and continue up the slope to reach the crown of **Small Down** by a gate at SU 676 206.

Turn right and wander along the broad crest of the hill that rewards with a glorious 360° panorama. It's one of the loveliest views to be had in the western Downs. ▶

Far off to the northeast can be seen the ridge of hills at Hindhead.

East Meon, with the tiny River Meon flowing through

The Small Down crest slopes downhill, where you go through a gate and continue to descend the slope to a woodland. Bear right along the edge of the woodland to a corner, then turn right to remain along the bottom of the meadow as far as the next corner. Now go through a gate where a clear path takes you briefly downhill among trees. Over a stile walk along the right-hand edge of a field, from where you can see a small cottage partially screened by pine trees slightly left ahead.

At the next corner go through a gap into the next field, and maintain direction through the centre. On the far side bear left along the headland towards Duncoombe Farm. Through a metal kissing gate wander down a sloping meadow to a second kissing gate which leads onto a narrow road opposite Princes Cottages on the edge of East Meon. Turn right and follow this into the heart of the village.

WALK 36

West Meon to Brockwood Copse

Distance	5 miles (8km)
Map	OS Explorer 132 Winchester 1:25,000
Start	West Meon church (SU 640 241)
Access	By bus from Winchester via Alresford, or from Petersfield. The village is on the A32, 1½ miles south of its junction with the A272
Parking	With discretion in the village
Refreshments	Pubs, café and shop in West Meon

Gathered on sloping ground in the fertile Meon valley, West Meon has a number of charming features, one of which is the pub whose name recalls Thomas Lord, the first owner of the famous cricket ground in London, who lies in the churchyard where this walk begins. It's an undemanding circuit through mostly arable farmland and woods; a gentle rolling landscape with footpaths, tracks and 'green lanes' flanked by trees and hedgerows lively with birds and small animals.

In the western end of the lower section of churchyard, just below the iron railings that divide the two levels, a stone stile in the boundary wall takes a footpath alongside a fence behind some houses, and on to the head of a road. Maintaining direction walk up the right-hand headland of a large field, and on reaching the far side go through a belt of trees and continue along the right-hand edge of a long meadow. This brings you to a very narrow lane at SU 626 237.

Turn right for a few paces, then immediately after passing Northend Cottage, fork half-left on a hedge-lined track marked on the 1:25,000 OS map as Bosenhill Lane. The walk remains on this track for a little over a mile along a seemingly never-ending woodland shaw, with a few rare views of large rolling farmland to the

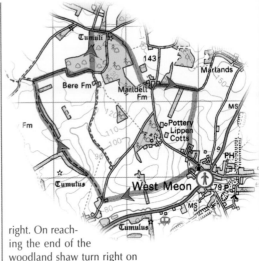

right. On reaching the end of the woodland shaw turn right on a crossing track shown as Green Lane on the 1:25,000 OS map.

Bordered by trees, the track leads to the woodland of Brockwood Copse where it turns sharply to the right, then left around the woodland edge. When the track makes a gentle curve to the right, take a footpath on the left. This takes you directly through the wood, then forks. Both branches lead out to a field on the north side of Brockwood Copse. Turn right along the field boundary which soon brings you to a narrow country road at SU 625 259.

Bear right and wander along the road for a short distance, then just before it curves left on the edge of the wood, leave it in favour of a footpath on the right which returns you to Brockwood Copse once more. This is an area of ancient woodland graced by handsome beech and oak trees, and the path remains close to its northeast edge, emerging to a lovely broad grass path. Keep ahead along this and eventually it will bring you to another narrow lane by **Marldell Farm**.

Bear left, but after a few paces turn right on a track among trees, then out between hedges. About ½ mile

after joining this track it makes a gentle left-hand bend. Leave it here by going through a gap in the right-hand hedgerow, and out to a surprise view across a folding landscape of fields and woods spreading through the Meon valley. Walk directly ahead on a broad path cutting through the middle of a large field. ▶

The path brings you along the back of some houses, then onto a road where you turn left, and soon wander past the parish church into the centre of **West Meon**.

May hedgerows are full with blossom

As you go down the slope, the first few buildings of West Meon may be seen below.

WALK 37

*West Meon to Old Winchester Hill
and Henwood Down*

Distance	9 miles (14.5km)
Map	OS Explorer 119 Meon Valley or 132 Winchester 1:25,000
Start	Station Road, West Meon (SU 641 238)
Access	By bus from Winchester via Alresford, or from Petersfield. The village is on the A32, 1½ miles south of its junction with the A272. Station Road is at the southern end of West Meon
Parking	At the start of the Meon Valley Trail (SU 642 236)
Refreshments	Pubs, café and shop in West Meon; drinks at Meon Springs Fly Fishery near Whitewool Farm

This fairly demanding walk begins easily enough by following the Meon Valley Trail along the bed of a former railway line, before making the ascent of Old Winchester Hill, the site of an Iron Age hillfort. After exploring country east of Old Winchester Hill, the route then climbs steeply onto the Downs above Drayton, and concludes with a mile-long walk alongside a road. Some sections of this counter-clockwise tour are used by the South Downs Way and the Monarch's Way; footpaths are clearly defined for the majority of the walk, and splendid views can be expected from a number of vantage points along the way.

Station Road filters away from the bottom end of West Meon's main street, and after passing a few houses, rises among trees. On coming to a narrow turning on the right, with a sign for the Meon Valley Railway, walk through a patch of woodland to reach a parking area at the start of the Meon Valley Trail which traces a section of this now dismantled railway. Bordered by trees and masses of rose-bay willowherb in a blaze of scarlet in summer, this easy pathway heads southwest along embankments and cuttings for about ¾ mile (1.2km). When you see a path slanting uphill on the right, wander up it and continue through

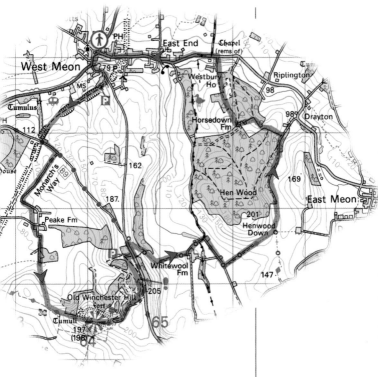

trees to
reach Old Winchester Hill Lane at SU 633 229.

The **Meon Valley Railway** between Alton and Fareham, was opened in 1903 as a link with the south coast, but it finally closed in 1968 after just 65 years of service. Its main claim to historic glory hangs on the fact that in a coach at Droxford station, south of West Meon, Allied commanders made their final preparations for the D-Day invasion of occupied France in June 1944. The 10-mile section of the dismantled line running from West Meon to Wickham has been given new life as a recreational route for walkers and cyclists.

Turn left, cross the railway bridge, and passing Hayden Farm wander along the lane until you come to a track on the right. Now follow this track heading southwest with a big open view which includes the tree-crowned Beacon Hill across the valley to the west, and Old Winchester Hill standing proud to the southeast. Used by the Monarch's Way, the track crosses the brow of a hill by a copse, then slopes downhill to curve left towards the buildings of **Peake Farm**.

On coming to the farmyard at Lower Peake, take a signed footpath on the right which crosses a footbridge and continues alongside a fence. After going between paddocks come onto a farm drive and bear left for a few paces, then right on a footpath beside a barn. Keep along the edge of a field and reach a concrete farm drive. When the concrete ends, continue ahead on the right branch of a track as far as a gate. Now veer left through a belt of trees, then turn right to wander uphill on the headland of a large field. At the upper right-hand corner continue up to a fence-line, then follow this round to the left to skirt a sloping meadow, at the top of which you come to a double signpost: one shows the route of the Monarch's Way, the other, the South Downs Way.

Turn left and walk up the left-hand side of a dividing hedge to reach the National Nature Reserve of **Old Winchester Hill**. Climbing among trees, pass through a kissing gate and go up to the summit of the hillfort to enjoy a wonderful 360 degree panoramic view that includes the Isle of Wight about 17 miles (27km) to the south.

The Iron Age **hillfort** on Old Winchester Hill covers an area of about 14 acres, and was built around 250BC when a Celtic tribe protected their homes with ramparts and a wooden palisade. But 1000 years or so before them, Bronze Age people buried their dead here in a series of round barrows that were excavated by Victorian archaeologists. The whole area contains a rich variety of wildlife and chalkland plants, and is now included within a National Nature Reserve of 150 acres.

Over the summit bear left on a crossing path which leads to a seat and an information board. To the right of these go through a gate and walk ahead: there are two parallel routes, a bridleway and an 'easy access route', both of which lead to a gate on the edge of a road. Do not go onto the road but turn left along the SDW bridleway which runs parallel with it. Pass another information board by a second gate giving access to the road, and maintain direction among bushes. Eventually a South Downs Way signpost directs you across the road, then through a gap in a hedge where you follow a fence-enclosed bridleway along the top edge of a meadow. This brings you to a point close to a road junction at SU 645 217.

Go through a bridle gate on the right and take a path cutting back to angle down and across the sloping meadow. At the bottom, pass through another gate near a small abandoned chalk pit, then bear left on a track between fields heading for **Whitewool Farm**. On coming to the farm buildings turn left round the edge of a flint-walled barn, then continue on the drive which takes

From Old Winchester Hill extensive views survey the Hampshire Downs

you past the front of the farmhouse, shortly after which you cross between small lakes of the Meon Springs Fly Fishery and come to a narrow road by another large farm building.

Follow this road to the right, and about 120 yards beyond Hall Cottage, turn left on a concrete farm road rising between fields. When the concrete ends a grass- and dirt-track continues ahead, now sloping downhill across the slopes of Henwood Down. On reaching a belt of trees and a crossing path, turn left onto what the 1:25,000 OS map calls Halnaker Lane.

At first through a woodland shaw, the way then goes along the edge of **Hen Wood** before cutting a little into the beechwoods. When it forks, take either branch as they reunite later and eventually bring you to a barrier. Beyond this continue on a track to reach the end of the woods. Now cross a stile on the left and climb a steep slope of meadowland; then over a second stile continue uphill beside the woods, but with ever expanding views to the north and northeast.

Reaching the crown of the hill, cross a stile on the left, and go through a patch of trees onto a stony track. Walk along the track which curves to the right and slopes downhill to a barrier. A few paces beyond, a signpost directs the continuing walk to the left where a narrow path climbs into a rough meadow. Keep along its right-hand edge, pass alongside a small corrugated barn or stable, and a few paces later veer right through a kissing gate (**Horsedown Farm** can be seen to the left).

Cross the farm drive and continue ahead through more woodland, then via another kissing gate out to a meadow. Turn right and wander down the slope before being drawn into woodland once more. At the bottom of the woods go through a gate and walk down the drive of **Westbury House** (a private nursing home) to a road. Turn left and follow this for 1 mile back to **West Meon**.

WALK 38

Exton to Warnford and Beacon Hill

Distance	6 miles (9.5km)
Map	OS Explorer 119 Meon Valley or 132 Winchester 1:25,000
Start	Exton Parish Church (SU 614 211)
Access	By bus from Bishops Waltham or Petersfield. Exton lies just off the A32, about 3 miles southwest of West Meon
Parking	With discretion in the village
Refreshments	Pubs in Exton and Warnford

Nestling in the Meon valley below Beacon Hill, Exton is a small village threaded by narrow lanes but thankfully spared the traffic of the nearby A32. Meaning 'the farmstead of the East Saxons' it's surrounded by pastures grazed by dairy herds, the meadows linked by footpaths that make this all fine walking country. This circular walk ventures both sides of the River Meon, and briefly visits Warnford, a neighbouring village with some of the watercress beds for which the river is justly famous, before climbing to the viewpoint of Beacon Hill and plunging back down the slope to Exton.

The peaceful River Meon on the outskirts of Exton

197

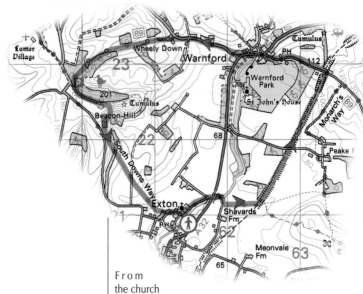

From
the church
of St Peter and St Paul in Exton, walk through the village towards the A32, passing to your right the road
which leads to The Shoe pub. A few paces beyond the
entrance to Manor Farm, note the pretty scene of the
River Meon on the right with moorhens dabbling in the
clear waters. Cross the A32 slightly left ahead to a path
signed for the South Downs Way. This crosses a footbridge over the Meon, and then is bordered by reeds
before curving to the right and coming to a track. After
a couple of paces turn left onto a narrow footpath from
which Old Winchester Hill can be seen ahead.

The path is drawn into a long woodland shaw with
an intermittent stream sometimes flowing through it. It's
a narrow path twisting among trees, and it leads to steps
which take you up onto the bed of an abandoned railway. Here you leave the South Downs Way and turn left
along the route of the unsigned Meon Valley Trail which
follows the old railway to West Meon, although we only
follow it for a little over 1¼ miles (2km). At one point

it's necessary to descend from an embankment to cross a narrow road leading to Peake Farm, then climb onto the railway path once more.

About 200 yards or so after passing beneath a road bridge, take a footpath cutting back on the left. Rising among trees it brings you to Old Winchester Hill Lane next to the bridge, where you turn right and wander along the road for about ½ mile (800m) to reach the A32 almost opposite The George and Falcon pub in **Warnford** (SU 624 232).

The trunk road through **Warnford** (A32) was originally built by French prisoners during the Napoleonic wars, which led to the village being moved ½ mile to its present position. To the south lie the ruins of the manor known as St John's House, after the family who lived there, with the isolated church of Our Lady nearby.

Cross the road with care, turn left and walk alongside the A32. Note the watercress beds beside the River Meon. Beyond these take the second turning on the right beside more watercress beds. Follow this country road for a little over ½ mile (800m), as far as **Wheely Down** Forge, where it curves to the right. Go left along a gravel drive towards Wheely Down Farm. After passing farm buildings curve right on a stony track rising uphill. This is used by the Monarch's Way. As you walk up this track, once again Old Winchester Hill can be seen across the valley, while the beech-crowned Beacon Hill rises ahead.

When the track forks take the right branch through a gate, then bear left along the edge of a meadow. A bridle gate takes the route forward alongside trees and bushes, with a deep basin containing a pond lying below Beacon Hill to the left. The way goes through a platt of hazelnut trees, then out to a large field giving extensive views to the left. Keep along the left-hand side of the field, then cross the stony track coming from Wheely Down Farm, and walk ahead into the woods of Beaconhill Beeches. The way soon emerges at a parking area beside a narrow road at SU 598 227.

The distant crest of Old Winchester Hill can be seen from Beacon Hill

Angle half-left through the car park to a gate where a South Downs Way sign indicates the way alongside the woods, now heading southeast with a hilltop field on your right. A few paces beyond the trig point marking the 659ft (201m) summit of **Beacon Hill**, curve right by a finger post to enjoy a panoramic view which includes the Isle of Wight to the south, Old Winchester Hill to the southeast, and Exton lying in the valley below.

Wander between fences down to a very narrow lane where you turn left, and a few paces later cross a stile on the left into a meadow. Bear right and follow the South Downs Way through a series of meadows linked by stiles all the way down to **Exton**. The route is well-marked, and it brings you at last through a metal kissing gate and a path leading to a road beside Glebe Cottage. Now wander down the road to the Parish Church in Exton.

WALK 39

Exton to Lomer Farm

Distance	6½ miles (10.5km)
Map	OS Explorer 119 Meon Valley or 132 Winchester 1:25,000
Start	Exton Parish Church (SU 614 211)
Access	By bus from Bishops Waltham or Petersfield. Exton lies just off the A32, about 3 miles southwest of West Meon
Parking	With discretion in the village
Refreshments	Pub in Exton

As is often the case when walking on the Downs, one gains the impression that this is a sparsely inhabited region, for there are long stretches where there are neither houses nor roads in sight, a landscape consisting of fields, meadows and woodland lying undisturbed. Of course, the land is worked and practically every square foot is used, but wandering through and across it, it's perfectly feasible to see no-one else for 90 per cent of the time. It's no wonder, then, that on this walk we pass the site of an abandoned village: no outlines of houses remain, no old bricks nor pieces of timber that once held a roof, just a few grassy humps where once villagers lived, laughed, loved and died, their community recorded in simple terms by the Ordnance Survey as 'Medieval Village of Lomer (site of)' ('Lomer Village' on the 1:50,000 map).

Leaving the Parish Church on your right, walk along the road a short distance, and after Glebe Cottage follow the South Downs Way as it goes along a track then footpath to a kissing gate leading into the first of a series of meadows that rise onto Beacon Hill. Walk along the right-hand side of this meadow, and when the boundary curves to the right, go through a gap then strike half-left across the next meadow to a stile in the bottom corner. Maintain direction to a double stile section either side of a semi-tangled strip of bushes, and continue in the same direction across the next meadow. Yet another stile in the boundary hedge takes the walk into another meadow, on the far side of which a good view can be had if you pause to look behind you.

Once again cross a stile, pass through a line of trees, then go up and across a steeply sloping meadow to another stile, after which the path maintains direction up to the top left-hand corner of a large sloping meadow (splendid views all the way) where a final stile gives onto a very narrow lane at SU 603 223. Turn right for a few paces, then right again where the SDW is led between fences to a bridle gate with a huge panoramic view to enjoy. Walk ahead for a very short distance to a finger post, then branch left to pass to the right of the trig post on **Beacon Hill**, beyond which a neat grass path goes alongside Beaconhill Beeches, then through a gate to a parking area and a narrow road.

Towards the western end of the Downs, **Beacon Hill** is one of several high points with this name, although it was formerly known as Lomer Beacon after the abandoned village whose site lies nearby. The slopes of this 659ft (201m) hill were worked by Celtic tribes, and traces of their field systems can still be seen on the

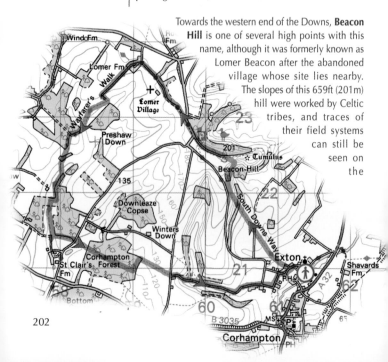

In mid summer cow parsley reaches full height on Beacon Hill above Exton

northeast flank. With its crown of beeches, Beacon Hill is protected as a National Nature Reserve, and it is said that 13 species of orchid can be found there.

Walk ahead along the road for about 250 yards. As it curves to the right go through a gate and continue along a track which takes you past Lomer Cottage (seen to the left), situated close to the site of the abandoned village, and keep on the track as far as a grain store at **Lomer Farm**. Turn left to pass between houses and a flint barn. The SDW branches right, but we take the left fork towards a timber-and-flint building, then follow a track along its left-hand side on the route of the Wayfarer's Walk.

Wandering along the track between fields come to a field gate with a stile beside it. Enter a large meadow with woods on the far side, go ahead for a few paces, then bear left round its boundary, wander down a slope to a woodland corner, then turn right. After walking alongside Rabbit Copse, go up a slope to a gap in the trees on the boundary ahead, where you leave the meadow by another stile next to a field gate, and onto a rising stony track. This goes alongside Preshaw Wood, in which (unseen from the route) there is a large earthwork, before coming to a crossing track. Bear left here, and when you reach the end of the wood, turn right along a field edge. When the woodland cuts back to the right, make your way half-left through the field to a stile on the edge of a small wooded area. ◄

Note the wild raspberries that grow next to the stile – a bonus to a walk in summer when the fruit is ripe.

Through the trees turn right along a field headland, and on reaching the corner, cross a stile in the hedge and turn left down the boundary of the next field, at the foot of which the area is known as Betty Mundy's Bottom. Turn right along the boundary towards a house marked on the map as Betty Mundy's Cottages. The way is then guided by a beech hedge around the boundary of this property, and into King's Copse. A neatly made path now leads on a circuitous tour (a few rustic bench seats beside the path) before dropping down to a gate at SU 578 217.

Through the gate enter a rough rectangular meadow bordered by woods. (The 1:25,000 map does not show this meadow, but depicts continuous woodland.) The path strikes directly ahead to a concrete farm drive. A few paces along this drive turn left onto a footpath which traces the left-hand edge of a sloping meadow beside a line of trees, from where you can see **St Clair's Farm** below to the right. In the far corner of the meadow go through a belt of trees and cross the very narrow Sailor's Lane.

Maintain direction through a woodland shaw, then at a crossing track walk ahead along the edge of **Corhampton Forest**. (Once again the 1:25,000 map ignores the field on the left, and shows this as continuous woodland.) When the left-hand field ends keep ahead on a forest track which ends in a rectangular clearing (again, unshown on the map). At the far side of this clearing turn left and enter the mixed woodland of Littleton Copse then, near the end of the wood, turn right and emerge into a large field.

Walk along the left headland as far as a gap in the left-hand boundary. Go through this, turn right and continue now along the right headland of a field which brings you to another narrow road opposite a track by Warner's Cottage. This slopes downhill to become a pleasant sunken track which eventually leads to a farm drive (Allens Farm Lane). Come to a road junction on the outskirts of **Exton**, and walk ahead to reach the centre of the village.

WALK 40

Cheriton to Tichborne

Distance	6½ miles (10.5km)
Map	OS Explorer 132 Winchester 1:25,000
Start	Cheriton Parish Church (SU 582 284)
Access	By bus from Winchester via Alresford, and from Petersfield via West Meon. Cheriton is on the B3046 about 3 miles south of Alresford
Parking	With discretion in the village
Refreshments	Pubs in Cheriton and Tichborne (200 yards off route)

The modest River Itchen rises among springs to the south of Cheriton, and flows northwards to Alresford before swinging west to Winchester and south to the sea. The stream brings a focus and adds character to Cheriton: it largely bypasses Tichborne, but that tiny village has plenty of character anyway, with its string of enchanting thatched cottages and pub, and the parkland of Tichborne House on the east bank of the young river. This walk explores a mixture of arable farmland and meadows on both sides of the Itchen, where the last of the South Downs spill into the Western Weald.

The parish church, with its squat brick tower, is found on the west side of the B3046 in the heart of Cheriton. Walk through the churchyard and out by its top right-hand corner, then cross a meadow towards the right-hand end of the village recreation ground. There you will find two stiles by the children's play area. Over these follow the left-hand boundary of a field as far as the next corner of the recreation ground. Now go through a gap on the left, cross a stile on the right and walk along the right-hand edge of a meadow. On reaching the top corner, go onto a farm drive and turn right. This brings you to a country road which you cross, and maintain direction on a narrow lane, soon rising gently before curving left between hedges.

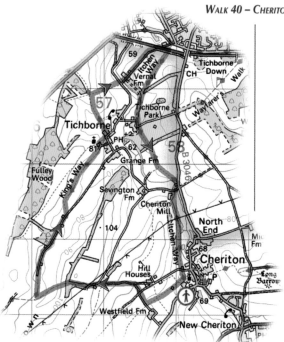

With big fields spreading on
either side of the lane, you eventually
come to the corner of a woodland. Leave the lane here
and enter the woods on a path which takes you through
to the far side. Leave by a bridle gate and wander down
the right-hand edge of a sloping meadow which forms
part of **Gander Down**. Keep ahead when the boundary
veers to the right, and approach the left-hand corner of a
hedge. On reaching this turn right and, with the hedge on
your left, walk towards a barn. Before reaching the barn
go through a gate and onto a track. ▶

Tichborne can be
seen in the
valley ahead.

Passing the barn, the track leads alongside another
woodland, beyond which there are two more barns: one
on the right, the other on the left. Shortly after passing
the left-hand barn, cross a stile in the left-hand hedge
and walk across a field to another stile in the opposite

207

boundary. Over this turn right and keep to the head-land which brings you into the next field with the tower of Tichborne church seen rising above the trees. Come to a sunken track which feeds into a narrow lane. Turn left up a slope to pass the entrance to the 11th-century church of St Andrew, then take a grass path between hedges on the right to reach a crossing track by a house at SU 570 304.

> **Note**
> Although the continuing walk turns left on this track, it would be worth making a brief diversion to the right onto the lane which runs through Tichborne village. Bear left along the lane where you'll find a string of charming thatched cottages and The Tichborne Arms pub.

Attractive thatched cottages are a feature of Tichborne

Turn left along the track which is soon flanked by hedges. Ignore an alternative track breaking to the right, and continue on what is marked on the map as **King's Way**. Wandering up a rise with the woodland of Trodd's Copse ahead, bear right then left through a gap into a field, where you turn right along its boundary, now sloping downhill alongside two fields to a narrow road at SU 573 311.

Cross directly ahead along a track/drive used by the Itchen Way, and within a few paces you cross the clear stream of the River Itchen. After passing farm buildings and a couple of houses, the way continues between fields. The track then narrows to a footpath running along the left-hand edge of a large field, before curving right between fences just above the A31 south of unseen Alresford. At the end of the field turn right through a gap among a few trees, then out to the large field around which you've been walking. Now heading southwest keep along its left-hand edge, go through a narrow strip of woodland and on to a track between trees ahead. This leads to a surfaced drive where you maintain direction through **Tichborne Park**.

As the drive turns sharply to the left, walk towards brick gateposts. Immediately before these cross a stile on the left, then turn right along the edge of a meadow. Through another woodland strip enter a large open field with a footpath cutting directly through it. A stile in the far boundary takes you into a second field, where the path strikes half-left in order to reach a country road. Bear right, and a few paces after passing a house, turn right again on a narrow road signed to Tichborne. ▶

Wandering along the road note that on the left lie the Itchen's water meadows.

Just after crossing the stream, turn left onto a drive that goes alongside **Cheriton Mill**. You then walk alongside a flint wall with the Itchen flowing on your left. Over a stile come into a sloping meadow and keep along its left-hand edge. A double stile in a hedgerow boundary leads into the next meadow where you maintain direction until coming to a narrow crossing lane. Directly ahead enter another meadow, across which you come to the churchyard in Cheriton where the walk began.

APPENDIX A
Route summary table

Walk	Title	Distance	Map	Start
1	Eastbourne to Birling Gap and East Dean	9½ miles (15km)	OS Explorer 123 1:25,000	Dukes Drive, Eastbourne
2	Butts Brow to Jevington and Friston	7 miles (11km)	OS Explorer 123 1:25,000	Butts Brow car park, Willingdon
3	Jevington to Friston Forest and the Long Man	7½ miles (12km)	OS Explorer 123 1:25,000	St Andrew's Church, Jevington
4	Jevington to Alfriston and Wilmington	8½ miles (13.5km)	OS Explorer 123 1:25,000	St Andrew's Church, Jevington
5	Exceat to East Dean and the Seven Sisters	8 miles (12.5km)	OS Explorer 123 1:25,000	Seven Sisters Country Park Visitor Centre, Exceat
6	Exceat to the Cuckmere Valley and Alfriston	7 miles (11km)	OS Explorer 123 1:25,000	Seven Sisters Country Park Visitor Centre, Exceat
7	Exceat Bridge to Cuckmere Haven and Seaford Head	6½ miles (10.5km)	OS Explorer 123 1:25,000	Golden Galleon pub, Exceat Bridge
8	Alfriston to The Long Man of Wilmington	5 miles (8km)	OS Explorer 123 1:25,000	River Lane, Alfriston
9	Alfriston to Bostal Hill, Alciston and Berwick	7 miles (11km)	OS Explorer 123 1:25,000	Star Lane, Alfriston

Walk	Title	Distance	Map	Start
10	Bopeep to Bishopstone	7½ miles (12km)	OS Explorer 123 1:25,000	Bopeep Car Park near Bostal Hill
11	Glynde to Beddingham Hill, Firle Beacon and Bostal Hill	11 miles (17.5km)	OS Explorer 123 1:25,000	Glynde Railway Station
12	Glynde to Mount Caburn and Saxon Cross	6 miles (9.5km)	OS Explorer 122 and 123 1:25,000	Glynde Railway Station
13	Southease Station to Rodmell and Telscombe	7½ miles (12km)	OS Explorer 122 1:25,000	Southease Station
14	Cooksbridge to Plumpton Plain and Buckland Bank	10 miles (16km)	OS Explorer 122 1:25,000	Cooksbridge Railway Station
15	Hassocks to the Clayton Windmills and Ditchling Beacon	10 miles (16km)	OS Explorer 122 1:25,000	Below Hassocks Railway Station on B2116
16	Devil's Dyke to Edburton Hill and Poynings	6½ miles (10.5km)	OS Explorer 122 1:25,000	Devil's Dyke Hotel
17	Devil's Dyke to Mile Oak Barn and Edburton Hill	6½ miles (10.5km)	OS Explorer 122 1:25,000	Devil's Dyke Hotel
18	Wiston to No Man's Land	6½ miles (10.5km)	OS Explorer 121 1:25,000	Chanctonbury Car Park
19	Findon to Cissbury Ring	7 miles (11km)	OS Explorer 121 1:25,000	The Square, Findon

Walk	Title	Distance	Map	Start
20	Washington to Chanctonbury Ring	4¾ miles (7.5km)	OS Explorer 121 1:25,000	Washington car park
21	Washington to Kithurst Hill	7½ miles (12km)	OS Explorer 121 1:25,000	The Street, Washington
22	Chantry Post to Myrtle Grove Farm	7 miles (11km)	OS Explorer 121 1:25,000	Chantry Post car park above Storrington
23	Storrington to Parham Park and Rackham Hill	7½ miles (12km)	OS Explorer 121 1:25,000	Amberley Road, Storrington
24	Amberley to The Burgh	6¾ miles (11km)	OS Explorer 121 1:25,000	Amberley Station
25	Burpham to Angmering Park	6 miles (9.5km)	OS Explorer 121 1:25,000	Burpham
26	Arundel to South Stoke and Burpham	8 miles (12.5km)	OS Explorer 121 1:25,000	Arundel High Street/Mill Road junction
27	Bignor Hill to Sutton	6¼ miles (10km)	OS Explorer 121 1:25,000	Bignor Hill car park
28	Bignor Hill to Slindon	7¾ miles (12.5km)	OS Explorer 121 1:25,000	Bignor Hill car park or Park Lane car park, Slindon
29	Duncton to Barlavington and Sutton	5 miles (8km) or 6 miles (9.5km) with Burton Mill Pond option	OS Explorer 121 1:25,000	Dye House Lane, Duncton or Burton Mill Pond car park

Walk	Title	Distance	Map	Start
30	Singleton to Littlewood Farm	5½ miles (8.8km)	OS Explorer 120 1:25,000	Singleton
31	West Stoke to Kingley Vale and Stoughton	6½ miles (10.5km)	OS Explorer 120 1:25,000	West Stoke car park
32	Compton to East Marden	5 miles (8km)	OS Explorer 120 1:25,000	The Coach and Horses, Compton
33	Harting Down to Beacon Hill and Telegraph House	5 miles (8km)	OS Explorer 120 1:25,000	Harting Down car park above South Harting
34	East Meon to Salt Hill	5 miles (8km)	OS Explorer 119 or 132 1:25,000	East Meon church
35	East Meon to Small Down	6 miles (9.5km)	OS Explorer 119 or 132 1:25,000	East Meon church
36	West Meon to Brockwood Copse	5 miles (8km)	OS Explorer 132 1:25,000	West Meon church
37	West Meon to Old Winchester Hill and Henwood Down	9 miles (14.5km)	OS Explorer 119 or 132 1:25,000	Station Road, West Meon
38	Exton to Warnford and Beacon Hill	6 miles (9.5km)	OS Explorer 119 or 132 1:25,000	Exton Parish Church
39	Exton to Lomer Farm	6½ miles (10.5km)	OS Explorer 119 or 132 1:25,000	Exton Parish Church
40	Cheriton to Tichborne	6½ miles (10.5km)	OS Explorer 132 1:25,000	Cheriton Parish Church

APPENDIX B
Useful addresses

INFORMATION
www.naturalengland.org.uk
www.visitsouthdowns.com
www.visitsussex.org
www.nationaltrust.org.uk

The Ramblers
2nd Floor, Camelford House
87–90 Albert Embankment
LONDON
SE1 7TW
☎ 020 7339 8500
www.ramblers.org.uk

Youth Hostels Association (England and Wales)
Trevelyan House
Dimple Road
MATLOCK
DE4 3YH
☎ 0800 0191 700
www.yha.org.uk

The South Downs Society
2 Swan Court, Station Rd.
PULBOROUGH
RH20 1RL
☎ 01798 875073
info@southdownsociety.org.uk

TOURIST INFORMATION CENTRES
61 High St
ARUNDEL
BN18 9AJ
☎ 01903 882268

Place St Maur
Belmont Street
BOGNOR REGIS
PO21 1BJ
☎ 01243 823140

10 Bartholomew Square
BRIGHTON
BN1 1JS
☎ 0906 711 2255 (calls cost 50p/minute)

96 Church Walk
BURGESS HILL
RH15 9AS
☎ 01444 238202

29a South Street
CHICHESTER
PO19 1AH
☎ 01243 775888

Cornfield Road
EASTBOURNE
BN21 4LQ
☎ 01323 411400

187 High Street
LEWES
BN7 2DE
☎ 01273 483448
lewes.tic@lewes.gov.uk

Look & Sea Centre
63-65 Surrey Street
LITTLEHAMPTON
BN17 5AW
☎ 01903 721866

Below Chanctonbury Ring a rewarding descent leads to Washington (Walk 20)

North Street
MIDHURST
GU29 9DW
☎ 01730 817322

The Library
27 The Square
PETERSFIELD
GU32 3HH
☎ 01730 268829

37 Church Street
SEAFORD
BN25 1HG
☎ 01323 897426
seaford.tic@lewes.gov.uk

The Guildhall
The Broadway
WINCHESTER
SO23 9LJ
☎ 01962 840500

Chapel Road
WORTHING
BN11 1HL
☎ 01903 221066

APPENDIX C
Bibliography

Illustrated Guide to Britain (AA/Drive Publications, 1974)

Bell, Quentin *Bloomsbury* (Weidenfeld and Nicolson, 1968)

Belloc, Hilaire *The County of Sussex* (Cassell, 1936)

Sonnets and Verses (c. 1954)

Brandon, Peter *The Sussex Landscape* (Hodder & Stoughton, 1974)

Darby, Ben *South Downs* (Robert Hale, 1976)

Harrison, David *Along the South Downs* (Cassell, 1958)

Hudson, WH *Nature in Downland* (London)

Jefferies, Richard *Nature near London* (1893, John Clare Books, 1980)

Mason, Oliver *South-East England* (Bartholomew, 1979)

Millimore, Paul *South Downs Way* (Aurum Press, 2001)

Moore, Christopher *The Green Roof of Sussex* (Middleton Press, 1984)

Nicolson, Adam *The National Trust Book of Long Walks* (The National Trust/Pan Books, 1981)

Pyatt, E *Chalkways of South and South East England* (David & Charles, 1974)

Reynolds, Kev *Classic Walks in Southern England* (Oxford Illustrated Press, 1990)

The South Downs Way (Cicerone Press, 2nd edition 2004)

Sankey, John *Nature Guide to South-East England* (Usborne, 1981)

Spence, Keith *The Companion Guide to Kent & Sussex* (Collins)

White, JT *The South-East, Down and Weald* (Eyre-Methuen)

The walk across the Seven Sisters is a much-loved outing (Walk 5)

NOTES

LISTING OF CICERONE GUIDES

For full and up-to-date information on our ever-expanding list of guides, visit our website: **www.cicerone.co.uk**.

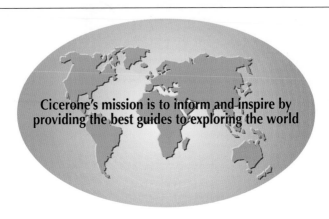

Cicerone's mission is to inform and inspire by providing the best guides to exploring the world

Since its foundation 40 years ago, Cicerone has specialised in publishing guidebooks and has built a reputation for quality and reliability. It now publishes nearly 300 guides to the major destinations for outdoor enthusiasts, including Europe, UK and the rest of the world.

Written by leading and committed specialists, Cicerone guides are recognised as the most authoritative. They are full of information, maps and illustrations so that the user can plan and complete a successful and safe trip or expedition – be it a long face climb, a walk over Lakeland fells, an alpine cycling tour, a Himalayan trek or a ramble in the countryside.

With a thorough introduction to assist planning, clear diagrams, maps and colour photographs to illustrate the terrain and route, and accurate and detailed text, Cicerone guides are designed for ease of use and access to the information.

If the facts on the ground change, or there is any aspect of a guide that you think we can improve, we are always delighted to hear from you.

Cicerone Press
2 Police Square Milnthorpe Cumbria LA7 7PY
Tel: 015395 62069 Fax: 015395 63417
info@cicerone.co.uk www.cicerone.co.uk